WHERE WOULD JOHN GO?
AMSTERDAM

ⓜ

Colophon

Where Would John Go? Amsterdam is a mo'media bv publication.
This book has been compiled and researched with a great deal of love, care and attention. However, some errors may have crept into the text. mo'media cannot be held responsible for these.
Reactions, complaints, and praise can be sent to mo'media, postbus 3936, 4800 DX Breda, The Netherlands,
info@momedia.nl
www.momedia.nl

All characters appearing in this work are fictitious. Any resemblance to real persons, living or dead, is purely coincidental.

Concept and design: Gummo (www.gummo.nl)
Words: William Georgi (www.willisgreat.co.uk)
Illustrations: Mattijs Werner and Hajo de Boer
Hustlers: Sterre Jongerius (Gummo) and Lisette Dirks (mo'media)
Lithography: MasterColors MediaFactory
Editor: Samantha van Kolck (mo'media)
With thanks to: The John Altman Organization (www.johnaltman.org)

ISBN 978-90-5767- 559-1
NUR 510
© mo'media bv, april 2012

All rights reserved. No part of this book may be reproduced or transmitted in any form or by any means, electronic, mechanical or otherwise, without the written permission of the publisher, except where permitted by law.

PUBLISHER'S NOTE

To forestall any disappointment, we would like to make it clear that John Altman did not write this book. This book was written by a man called William Georgi. Or William Thomas Francis Georgi, as his mum calls him when she's not pleased with him. William, or Will, as his friends know him, is from London. He's lived in the Netherlands for five years and in Amsterdam for the last three. And he's not John Altman.

This book is inspired by what Will learned from John and the founders of the John Altman Organisation, two Dutchmen called Hajo and Onno. That's why it's called *Where Would John Go*, not *Where Would I Go*, or *Where Did John Go*.
We know John's been to Amsterdam and we know he likes it very much, as when he found out Hajo and Onno lived there, he embraced them to his heart (he embraced everyone to his heart) took them into his home (he didn't take everyone into his home) and they spent many hours reminiscing about a city they both loved.

So if you read a sentence that begins *I went,* then it's somewhere Will went. And if it's *we went...* it's somewhere Will or his friends in the John Altman Organisation went. And if it's *John went,* well, it's somewhere John went.

Got it? Good. Then let's go!

WHERE WOULD JOHN GO?

CONTENTS

WHO IS JOHN ALTMAN? *(Introducing you to the man, the myth, the legend that is Mr. John Altman)* 6

DOING NOTHING
(That explains how doing less on holiday gets more done) 10

GOING DUTCH
(That explains how to communicate successfully with the locals) 20

OOST, WEST, THUIS BEST *(That explains where John would stay in Amsterdam. Or at least tries to)* 30

DOING NOTHING OUTSIDE *(That shows you how not to let the elements get in the way of doing nothing)* 44

DOING NOTHING INSIDE *(That mainly concerns one of the hardest Dutch words to say that's not Scheveningen)* 58

FIETSEN
(Or how my mum learned to stop worrying and love the bike) 74

WATER *(That's where it's at in Amsterdam)* 90

EEN BROODJE WARM VLEES EN PINDASAUS *(That's a warm meat and peanut sauce roll, and that explains how doing (or eating) nothing is the key to eating well in Amsterdam)* 106

WHERE JOHN WOULDN'T GO *(That tells you how to get out of a tight spot and shows you some much nicer places to do nothing rather than something)* 124

WHERE WOULD JOHN GO?
(That contains some helpful names and numbers) 140

Who is John Altman?
(Introducing you to the man, the myth, the legend that is Mr. John Altman)

Well, to most people he's the dude with a beard and a winning smile who bakes their favourite cookies. To some people, he's the go-to guy whenever you're looking for a good bottle of wine. But for us, John's simply the friend we made when we bumped into him all those years ago in San Francisco. Back then he was just a man wearing an apron (and not much else) giving away cookies on Baker Beach.

It might have been the sun, it might have been the gentle sea breeze or it might just have been the intense combination of melted butterscotch and freshly squeezed grapefruit, but they were the best cookies we'd ever tasted. So damn good that we had to ask John if we could have the recipe. "Sure dude," he said, "spread the love!"

So that's exactly what we did. Well, that's exactly what we did after we spent a week at his house chilling out, maxing, relaxing all cool and shoot-

ing a little b-ball outside of his pool. And in the moments in-between, he baked, we ate and John gave us his blessing to spread the love around the globe.

What we learned in our short time together inspired us to set up the John Altman Organisation; an organisation dedicated to spreading the word of John (and the love) in his absence. Yes, in his absence, since as hard as we've tried (and we've tried hard, believe us) we've never been able to re-establish contact with John.

Therefore all we can tell you with any certainty about John is that he's got a penchant for bandanas, possibly developed during a stint roadying for a particularly progressive rock band back in the day. He lives (or lived) in San Francisco. He's a dab hand in the kitchen. He likes travelling. He doesn't like wearing clothes. He was particularly proud of a signed copy of *What's Going On* that he was given by Marvin himself and had an endearing habit of hugging everyone he met. And his best friend was a man called Yogi Bear who offered courses in meditation that consisted mainly of lying around in the sun and contemplating nature over several glasses of wine.

Since John is no longer part of our daily lives, everything we do is therefore our attempt to keep his spirit alive and share the values that he instilled in us with the rest of the world. To love people (or do your best to try). To love the planet. To spread that love as far and wide as you can. And have as much fun doing it as possible - that's what John would do.

It's pretty straightfoward, as almost everything is with John. Especially if you follow his other philosophical gift to the human race: do less, get more done. It sounds good, doesn't it? Well, we're just about to get right into it.

WHO IS JOHN ALTMAN?

Doing NOTHING
(That explains how doing less on holiday gets more done)

Do less, get more done. Now, John Altman has said, and made, a lot of life-enhancing things, but this majestic monument to inactivity will always remain one of his greatest achievements; a quote, nay, an ethos that elevates him to the sort of status that should see statues erected in his honour and a few thousand babies named after him.

John first stumbled across the manifold possibilities of inactivity due to its integral role in the baking process. Yet as with so much of what John taught us, we found it was a lesson as relevant in life as in the kitchen. Quite simply what it boils down to is doing less of the stupid, pointless things that eat up so much of our time and more good things instead.

John figured, quite wisely as it turned out, that it's more fulfilling to do one thing well than to try and do ten things simultaneously badly. So that means less worrying about small details, less multitasking, less checking emails on your mobile phone, less mobile phone, period. More focusing on stuff you really want to do, whether it's baking a cookie, listening to a record or enjoying your holiday. That's how you do less and get more accomplished.

Goodness knows it's a philosophy we need to take onboard because if there's one luxury in today's world, it's time. We

THINGS THAT SOMEONE FROM Amsterdam would NEVER do.

Well, the easy answer is a whore.
Another one would be leaving Amsterdam. Because if you live in Amsterdam, you're convinced that it's the greatest place to live in the whole wide world. Despite the fact that The Netherlands' generally excellent (and relatively cheap) public transport system makes much of the country easily accessible, getting Amsterdammers out of Amsterdam is as difficult as parting them from their money. That's partly because Amsterdam really is the best place in the Netherlands but also because they're ever so slightly lazy. Within Amsterdam even a short trip across town assumes such epic proportions that the journey will be abandoned before they even step outside, in favour of staying at home and eating hutspot. In other words, doing nothing.

have even less of it than money and that's saying something in 2012. We rush to work, we spend most of the day at work, we rush home and in between we try and cram as much activity as humanly possible into every second of every day. Yet somehow we're still surprised when we end up with less 'free' time at the end of the day. That's precisely why we go travelling, to break this cycle and do something completely different. But even on these God-given chances to do nothing we still feel the need to try and cram as much activity into our vacation as possible.

Take for example two of my best friends, Bas and Femke (their names have been changed to protect their identities). Every second of their 'holiday' is regulated by a strict regime that involves waking up every morning at 7.30 am (precisely) before proceeding to every museum and point of vague interest within a three kilometre radius of their hotel until they drop from exhaustion. Their itinerary is so rigid that it doesn't even allow for a quick trip to the restroom (I love that word) unless it's in the scheduled five minute pause. I love Bas and Femke dearly but I'd never go on holiday with them. I mean, that sort of holiday is all well and good if that's your thing, but that's not what doing nothing is about. Hell, that shouldn't be what doing anything is about.

What John wants out of a holiday is pretty simple. To meet new people. See new things. Mainly he just wants to have a good time and to feel at home. And the best way to do this, he reasons, is to do what the locals do. And what the locals do, most of the time, is nothing. After all, when you're at home, do you go round rushing round museums, looking round churches and queuing outside tourist attractions? Of course you don't. You might do it every once in a while, but then when you do embark on such a trip, you do it because you really, really want to and you make a special day out of it. Doing less, to get more done, you dig?

But wait, I hear you cry, I WANT to do lots of things in Amsterdam! I want to see the sights, I want to go the museums, I want to experience everything that makes Amsterdam unique and worth coming here in the first place. Rest assured, you can do that. And more, if you absolutely insist. But that's not what we really mean by doing nothing. It's a question of balancing your desire to see the most things possible against the danger of missing the bigger picture.

For example. One of my favourite cities in the world is La Paz in Bolivia. I was only there for three days and all I did there was nothing. Okay, I did cycle down the world's most dangerous road, get mugged, have a chance encounter with three drug dealers and run from two gentleman purporting to be policeman whose grasp of Bolivian law seemed to be even shakier than mine. But that aside, I did nothing apart from watch football in a bar, drink a lot of beer and stroll around town with my brother marvelling at one of the most beautiful, fascinating, alive and intriguing cities in the world. That's exactly the way that we want you to feel about Amsterdam after your trip: for you to arrive home proudly telling anyone who will listen that it's your new favourite place in the whole

Other books on Amsterdam

Other books on Amsterdam? Pff, why would you bother? You've obviously got the best book about the city in your hands, so instead of wasting both of our time with listing other inferior books, we'll give you a few names to shed some further light on the character of the city before you come.

The Amsterdam of Theo van den Boogaard. This is a brilliant book based on the comic strips drawn for the legendary Amsterdam character Sjef van Oekel. Sjef was a man dressed in a bowtie and dinner jacket who found himself caught up in a variety of escapades around Amsterdam that inevitably involved Amsterdam's ladies of night. The comic was the brainchild of Wim T Schippers, one of the Netherlands' most, um, special artistic talents. His greatest hit was undoubtedly the 'Peanut Butter Floor' – a floor covered in peanut butter – a feat he topped only by managing to sell the floor (or at least the concept) to another museum.

Amsterdam: The Brief Life of a City by Geert Mak. Geert is the Mak Daddy of Amsterdam History and this is his masterwork.

Anything by Johannes van Dam. This dude is the main restaurant critic in Amsterdam, the dude whose review can make or break a restaurant in the city, who can turn you into the hottest place in town or drive you into bankruptcy. Really, the guy in "Ratatouille" has nothing on him. He writes for the local newspaper, the Parool, which is in Dutch, as is his regular collection of reviews in "Lekker Amsterdam". So if you want to know which tent is top, the easiest thing to do is just ask your friendly Amsterdam friend what Mr van Dam is up to.

And where to buy these books? At one of the bookshops indicated in the handy diagram below, of course!

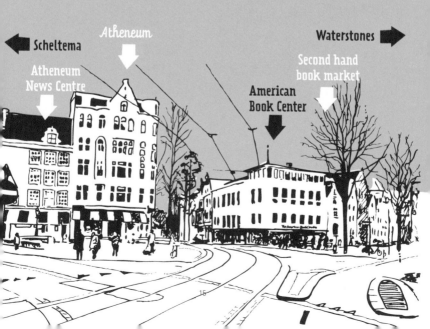

world. And for that to happen, all you have to do is read this book (and go to Amsterdam).

The first time I came to Amsterdam I was 18. I arrived via the sleeper train from Vienna and emerged blinking into the sunlight onto the plaza outside Centraal Station. Being eighteen, and English, my friend and I headed down what I now know as the Singel in search of a coffeeshop.

One of the first things we saw was a gentleman lying unconscious on the pavement. I thought, well, maybe this is the city for me.

Coffeeshops
Sadly it would appear that no book about Amsterdam is complete without a section on coffeeshops. No, not places that sell coffee, but the places that sell weed. We could quite easily have fitted them into the bit about 'Things People From Amsterdam Would Never Do' but John taught us never to disappoint your public. The thing is that while coffeeshops do have obvious advantages, they're just not that appealing unless you're a big fan of reggae being played really loudly and dodgy décor featuring aliens and giant ganja leaves. Salubrious, I believe the word is.
So if you really want to get your smoke on, I'd suggest you take your weed away and enjoy it in the comfort of your own home as the great majority of people here do. Or head to West Amsterdam to one of the Moroccan cafés that serve flavoured tobacco in water pipes. It's a thoroughly pleasant way to spend an hour or two and the food is decidedly better than in the majority of the other coffeeshops.

It would be some seven years before I experienced the delights of Amsterdam again and I have to confess that I wasn't exactly enamoured upon my return. At that point I was living elsewhere in the Netherlands (Utrecht, since you ask, a town also worthy of your investigation) and I'd come to Amsterdam to go to concerts at Paradiso or the Melkweg.

So I'd arrive at the train station, get the tram down Damrak to Leidseplein, go the gig then go home. And if there are two places you don't really want to be in Amsterdam, it's the Damrak or Leidseplein (even if you do want to go to Paradiso) as they're as close to hell as Amsterdam gets.
Thus scarred by my encounters with Amsterdam's own versions of Sodom and Gomorrah, I avoided the city like the plague until I was fortunate enough to make some Dutch friends who showed me that there was more to Amsterdam than that godforsaken strip of coffeeshops and titty bars. A few years down the line and Amsterdam has become, well, home to me, all thanks to the people that I've been privileged to meet along the way.

I didn't know any better about Amsterdam when I first came here because I had no one to turn to for advice in those dark days before a book as well-written and extensively researched as this one was available. Back then there was no John to tell me to avoid Rembrandtplein, no John to show me which end of a herring to put in your mouth first (remarkably it's not the one with the tail) and no John to advise me on the best Dutch words to drop in conversation to make friends and influence people. Because as John drummed into us, it's friends, and friendly advice, that remain the best way to find your way around a city, and get through life in fact.

In this book we'll give you the best start we can to help you hit the ground running when you get here, but after that, you're on your own. Not (just) because we're too lazy to do otherwise, but because we think it would be wrong. One of the joys of travelling is that heady feeling engendered by discovering things for yourselves - wandering down that side alley to find that special rooftop restaurant, that bar you're drawn into because of the funny name or the hot waitress. Whatever or wherever it is, it's special because it's something you've found yourself and not through a book.

Like that street food shack in the middle of nowhere we ended up at in Marrakech. They only spoke Arabic and somehow my ever so slightly Creole-accented French didn't cut the mustard so we resorted to good old-fashioned pointing, gesturing wildly and playing the 'tell us what animal is in the soup game' by getting down on our knees and mooing. (In Amsterdam a cow goes *boe* for future reference.) But whether that café was a true representation of the city or not, we were left with the distinct impression that we'd had a taste of the 'real' Marrakech, instead of the touristy bits (although what we tasted in the soup, we're still not quite sure). Whatever it was, it's memories like these that make travelling special.

And you'll be pleased to hear that even though you're not in Amsterdam yet, doing nothing starts right here, right now. In fact, by taking a bit of time out for yourself and reading this book, you're already having a taste of the good times that await you in Amsterdam. How? Simply by removing all other distractions, settling down with a warming drink and this book, that's how. And to bring Amsterdam even closer to you, we're going to introduce you to the best way to make yourself feel at home there - by trying to speak a little Dutch of course. It's not quite as bad as it sounds, honestly…

Going Dutch
(That explains how to communicate successfully with the locals)

It's well known that the Dutch speak excellent English. They're justifiably proud of their foreign language skills and will happily seize any opportunity to demonstrate their prowess in the language of Shakespeare, Orwell and Georgi. However, you shouldn't assume that this allows you to speak English with impunity in Amsterdam. Because, well, it wouldn't be very polite of you and besides, if you try to learn even just a few words of their language, the Dutch will love you for it. And as Dutch is part of the same language group as English and German, it's really not that hard to pick up if you already speak one of those two languages.

The Dutch would say that by sitting on top of the Royal Palace on Dam square John is being as 'crazy as a door'. John would say he doesn't give a dam.

N.B. If you're going to compare Dutch to any language, it shouldn't be German. No way, as the Dutch aren't the biggest fans of their neighbours. The cause for this is much of a muchness with the same rivalry caused by close proximity that means the Scots hate the English, the Norwegians hate the Swedes, Canadians resent Americans and everyone in South America despises the Argentines. But the recent tension between the Dutch and the Germans is mostly about the Second World War and football (losing a World Cup Final is a hard thing to take). Which means that if you feel, like a friend of mine, drawn into making a comparison between the two countries, you'll be greeted rather coldly. Especially if you decide to do this in the middle of a crowded supermarket. And what you say goes something along the lines of "Basically, Holland's just like Germany, isn't it?" Silence ensued as everyone, but everyone, swivelled in our direction. In order to dispel the tension, I gamely (and somewhat lamely) offered up the classic defence of "I don't know what you're talking about, they're completely different and anyway isn't everything much better here than in Germany, etc, etc." This and other similarly obsequious comments were enough to placate the bloodthirsty crowd until my friend blithely wittered on: "Nah, I mean, they look the same, they cook the same, they speak the same…" The rest of his monologue was lost in a sea of potatoes, carrots and cauliflowers as we were forced to exit the supermarket pretty damn sharp. The fact that my friend might have had a point is irrelevant, you just can't go around making these sorts of comments in Amsterdam and expect to make any friends.
Note Over.

Anyway, to get back to speaking Dutch, the hardest thing about learning it is actually trying to get the words out. You've probably already heard about the infamous Dutch 'g', a sound for which you need summon up every bit of phlegm lodged in your throat before swiftly projecting it (the sound, not your phlegm) out of your mouth whilst trying to say 'kkkhhh.' And as if that wasn't hard enough, you've then got to master the vowels, most of which require you to contort your face into a variety of uncomfortable positions in order to come anywhere near to pronouncing them properly. Sadly all this effort will go to waste, as the excessive gurning and level of spittle you'll have to expel to produce even the first 'g' of *goeiemorgen* ('good morning') will immediately alert your audience to your status as a foreigner. Still, they'll appreciate your effort and will reward you for it by speaking flawless English back to you.

If, however, your 'g' does pass muster (congratulations!) that means you've probably been taken for either a Belgian, German, South African or someone Dutch who's a couple of slices of cheese short of a sandwich - you can pick which category you find the most flattering yourself. As no matter how good your 'g' is, there'll be something else you haven't got quite right - there always is, it's just a hard language to master. However, the Dutch are incredibly patient with any attempts you make to speak their language, a stance that significantly softens the blow of having to confront your inability to say even the simplest of Dutch words correctly. And even if, years later, you master the language, trying to get your head round how the Dutch communicate with each other is just as mind-boggling.

To say they're direct, well, would be to tell the truth. Let's take a random scenario. Say, for example, you want to phone a friend to ask them a favour. In most countries you'll make small talk for a little bit before getting round to whatever it is you really want to discuss. But Amsterdam isn't 'most countries'. Dutch people will just jump in there and ask for what they want right away, no matter what it is or how well they know you. The Dutch speak their mind in a way that other people simply don't. So if they want to ask you something, they will. Just like that. Bam.

A typical conversation on the phone with them will go a little something like this:
'Rogier speaking.' (No one Dutch says 'Hello' on the phone, just 'Met (your name)' which means 'with Rogier.' Nope, I don't get it either. And they think we're rude for simply saying 'Hello' when we answer the phone.)
'Hi Rog, it's Sjam.'
'Hello Sjam.'
'Can I borrow fifty thousand Euros from you?' (You don't have to say please in Dutch, just saying 'Can I', or 'May I', is considered polite enough. Saying please is just going over the top.)
'Er, no.'
'Okay Rog, no hard feelings, thanks buddy. See you soon.'
'Bye.' Rog hangs up.
'Tosser.'

If you're slightly shocked by the nature of this conversation, I'm afraid this rather brusque exchange encapsulates how the

Dutch communicate with each other: directly and with almost no subject considered taboo. Like money for example. In most of the civilised world, asking someone how much they paid for something or how much they earn is a huge conversational no-no. In Amsterdam it's considered perfectly acceptable, a simple matter of interest on the same level as asking whether you enjoyed the meal or what the weather was like while you were on holiday.

This 'openness' isn't confined to taboos such as money. Personal details and features are also considered fair game. Not long after my arrival in Holland, I got talking to a Dutch girl in a bar. I had the distinct impression that things were progressing nicely between us, an impression confirmed when the girl leaned in and whispered: "So, I suppose you think you're tall, don't you?" - a question right up there with "Have you been working out?" in the "Do you want to go to bed with me?" stakes. In response to her unmistakable overtures, I pumped up my chest, drew myself up to my full six foot one inches and a half (that's 185 cm for our metric friends) and said "Well, yes, I suppose I am" with what I hoped was the right mix of charm and modesty to seal the deal. "No," came her answer, "you're not. In this country you're just average." At which point she walked away, leaving me to pick my jaw and dignity off the floor. Welcome to Amsterdam.

Even the Dutch friends you make over here won't hold back on the flagellating criticism. One of my very best friends, someone who hasn't got a bad word to say about anyone (except me, it transpires) informed me earnestly that I have a "fucked up" face. My asymmetric face fell apart even further upon hearing this, despite her assurances that she meant it "nicely". To say that her words have haunted me ever since wouldn't, for once, be a gross exaggeration.

However you'll be relieved to hear that, directness and pronunciation issues aside, communicating with people in Amsterdam is a piece of cake. Or *een stukje taart* as they say here. As we already touched upon, everybody here speaks English and is used to communicating with English speaking people. And as you're obviously at home enough with the English language to enjoy this book, you shouldn't have any problems getting by in Amsterdam.

Especially if you master the following key Dutch words we've picked out to give you a head start in the language. Good luck!

A IS FOR 'ALSJEBLIEFT'.
Pronounced 'al-sh-beleaved' (well, almost).
Alsjeblieft means please or 'there you go.' Using it upon requesting something will establish you immediately as a polite person and therefore a very good person to know. It's the quickest way to make friends and influence people in the Dutch language.

D IS FOR 'DANK JE'
Pronounced 'dank yeh'
We told you Dutch wasn't hard to learn. Well, *dank je* is the living proof of this. Many Dutch words are identical to English ones – man, water, compact disc – and even more are only a couple of letters different, like *dank je*, which means 'thank you.' Which is nice and easy to say and nice and easy to use too. Which in our book is a win-win situation.

F IS FOR 'FIETS'
Pronounced 'feets'
A *fiets* is a bike. And a bike is your best friend in Amsterdam, as you'll find out in the chapter that we've devoted to this princely form of transport. The b in bike stands for brilliant, trust us.

G IS FOR 'GEZELLIG'
Pronounced 'kh (this is the throat clearing sound we were talking about earlier)' zel-ik-kh (more throat clearing if you can manage it, please).

We're going to be talking a lot about this word in the chapter on doing nothing inside. It's an important word, so for now we'll just ask you to practice saying it. 'Kh-zel-ik-kh.' It just rolls off the tongue, doesn't it?

G IS FOR 'GRATIS'
Pronounced 'gra-tis'
Gratis is the Dutch, well, the Latin word originally, for free. Without cost. As in you don't have to pay anything for something. The phrase there's no such thing as a 'free lunch' is no more apposite than in Amsterdam. The Dutch reputation for watching every penny and cent is sadly justified and therefore the chances of seeing anything gratis during your time here are highly unlikely and thus must be seized upon with enthusiasm, especially if it's *gratis bier* which means free beer.

H IS FOR HOOFDDEKSEL.
Pronounced 'ho-fff-deck-sell'
Hoofddeksel isn't a word you're likely to use during your time in Amsterdam. But it is useful in illustrating the charming intricacies of the Dutch language. *Hoofddeksel*, you see, means 'hat'. Literally translated into English it means 'head lid,' a piece of reasoning that is undeniably logical and endlessly amusing, at least for me.

L IS FOR LEKKER

Pronounced 'leck-ker'

Another word you'll get a lot of mileage out of. *Lekker* means 'tasty' when appraising food and 'foxy' for people. Either way it should be used with relish.

M IS FOR 'MAG IK?'

Pronounced 'mach ick'

These two words hold the key to getting whatever you want in Amsterdam, for *mag ik* means 'may I?' Therefore all you have to do to obtain any object of your desire is say *'Mag ik?'* point at said object of desire, give the possessor of said object of desire a winning smile and the thumbs up, and said object of desire will be yours.

Oh yes, it will be yours.

S IS FOR SCHEVENINGEN

Pronounced – Lord knows how it's pronounced, sorry, for Scheveningen is the hardest word to pronounce in the Dutch language. What we can tell you is that it's a beach resort near The Hague, and Dutch people used it as a test during the war to see if strangers really were Dutch or not, because if you were Dutch you could say it, and if not, well, you couldn't.

S IS FOR 'SORRY'

Pronounced 'sorry'

Except it's not. Pronounced 'sorry' as in the English manner I mean. It does mean exactly the same in Dutch as it does in English but somehow it's pronounced in a subtly different manner. No matter how close you think you get to the correct pronunciation of this word, Dutch people always identify it as being foreign. It's a mystery. Maybe it's just the fact that you're apologizing for something - something that the Dutch don't really do. However this a subject perhaps best addressed in another book, one in which John goes to London most likely.

Oost, West, Thuis Best

(That explains where John would stay in Amsterdam. Or at least tries to)

It won't surprise you to learn that John wasn't really fussy about where he slept at night. Give him a pillow, a blanket and somewhere to lay his head and he'd be fine. No matter whether it was a spot on a park bench or the swankiest hotel in town, he'd call both home. For John, it was all about the vibe. If a place felt right, well, that was more than good enough for him.

Of course, that's all very nice and easy for us to say from the comfort of our easy chairs in Amsterdam, and not much help to you when you're trying to find a place to call home during your stay here.

The good news is it really doesn't matter that much where you stay in Amsterdam. One of this city's main attractions is that it's by and large a jolly nice city and quite a small city too (with just under a million people living here) so you'll never be far from anywhere that's even more pleasant than where you are.

Amsterdam's compact size also lends the city much of its charm, as it makes it possible for you to bump into your friends and acquaintances all the time. Okay, maybe not all the time, but much more often that you would in a 'real' city. In London, for example, if you spot someone you think you recognise, you'll probably dismiss it, thinking 'Wow, that girl really looks like Juultje' because the odds of chancing upon

Juultje at that time
of day in that part
of town are so remote
that you'd be more likely
to bump into John himself. And, as
you'd be so busy doing whatever you have to
do that's so pressing that you walk at breakneck speed to
get wherever you need to be in London, you probably wouldn't
have time to stop and chat anyway. But in Amsterdam, it will
be that person, because, well, it invariably is. And you will have
time to stop and chat, because, well, everyone always does.

It's said that most cities have six degrees of separation, but
here's it's just one. Which is a gift and a curse, but mainly a
gift. On a good day, when you're running into your friends left,
right and centre, it makes the city feel like one big episode of
Cheers, a place where everybody really does know your name.
Combine this with all the cultural attractions of a 'proper' metropolis, but on a much more intimate scale (both personally
and geographically) where everything's only a twenty minute
cycle ride away, and you begin to understand why Amsterdam
is such a special place.

It is, as some people in the marketing trade like to call it, a
village metropolis. I'd prefer to say it's just a nice place to be.
A place that's welcoming, fulfilling and entertaining in equal

measure. That's not to say it's perfect, but stay here for longer than a day and you'll soon understand why it scores highly on those ridiculous quality of life surveys.

But where to stay, hey? That's the question. Even in a city as consistently wonderful as Amsterdam there are different shades of perfection. Here's our guide to some of the parts of town where John would (and wouldn't) go.

THAT BEGINS BY TELLING YOU ABOUT A HOUSING SYSTEM THAT YOU PROBABLY WON'T HAVE ANYTHING TO DO WITH BUT IS STILL PRETTY INTERESTING

At this point in the book you'd probably expect some form of concrete, practical advice on where to stay in Amsterdam. After all, it's probably one of the most important things to sort out for your trip. Well, that's not quite how we roll, I'm afraid. The people who you should never ask where to stay in a city are the people who live there. Because let's face it, unless you're in Buenos Aires and looking for a place to go for half an hour with your special someone, you're not likely to ever avail yourself of a hotel's service. And anyway, round here people go to Breukelen for that (yes, the village a stone's throw from Amsterdam that gave the NY borough its name, just like another village outside the city called Haarlem). To Hotel Breukelen, if you really want to know, the bizarre Chinese style building just outside the town. Get the slow train to Utrecht, you can't miss it.

To be fair, we did try and do some research in this area (on where to stay in Amsterdam, not on love hotels) but surprisingly rolling up to a hotel and informing the highly sceptical manager that you're writing a travel guide and could I possibly have a free room for the night and maybe a free meal and unlimited minibar access too, doesn't wash with the majority of Amsterdam hoteliers. None, in fact. Not even if you say please. But what we can, and will, happily do is point you in the general direction of a couple of handy places in which you can secure, er, alternative accommodation. And authentic Amsterdam accommodation at that. All in all, the kind of places where John would stay.

One method of finding a bed for the night that John would make frequent use of is couchsurfing, the global network of people happy to offer free accommodation for no reward apart from good karma. To avail yourself of this quite wonderful service, all you need to do is create a profile on the website, say something nice about yourself, then, bam, you've got yourself a free spot on a sofa.

Another, perhaps more luxurious, option is house swapping. We'd recommend the house of a good friend of John's, a certain O. Lixenberg, the proud owner of a palatial suite in the Jordaan if you'd like to stay somewhere really special. But the best option, the most exciting, cheapest and, the most 'Amsterdam' thing to do, is to squat somewhere. No, not to get down on your haunches in the middle of the street, but to occupy a vacant building. Or *kraken* as they call it in Dutch.

There's a long and glorious tradition in Holland of people taking advantage of any empty or abandoned building space and making their home there. The legality of the system is hazy at best (actually it's not, it's been properly illegal for the last couple of years) but in the good old days if you could claim that there was an open window and you hadn't forced your way into the house, you just happened to find your way in, then you might be on the right side of the law. And if that didn't work, you could try offering the perennial excuse that you're a foreigner and didn't know any better. Anyway, this system has seen large chunks of the city being krakked, like in the Spuistraat in the centre of Amsterdam, where most of the buildings with graffiti murals on the exterior are kraakhouses (it's a copywriter's dream this kraak thing. It's almost as addictive as, oh, okay, we'll leave that one there).

Of course, this sort of accommodation might be slightly harder for the casual tourist to come by, but that doesn't mean you should totally rule it out. If you want to meet some truly interesting people, in some truly interesting places, then there's nowhere better to be. Although you shouldn't probably hang around these buildings asking if you can come in, as you might be taken for a policeman or, heaven forbid, a representative of the 'man' but drop John's name, or even better, some of his cookies, and who knows where you'll end up.

Maybe somewhere like my friend's kraakhouse, where he has a floor, yes, a whole floor of an office with about ten rooms all to himself. That's impressive enough in itself, and that's before I tell you that he has access to a roof that's bigger than most flats

in Amsterdam with a view over the city to die for (and with enough room to fit forty people for a barbecue). And all this is 100% street legal and comes with the added (and not inconsiderable) thrill of sleeping in an office. It's the Altman dream in excelsis. Hallelujah!

HOUSEBOATS

A more realistic, yet equally attractive, form of accommodation in Amsterdam is the houseboat. In other countries these are known as barges, and some houseboats are indeed old barges, but in Amsterdam they've taken it a step further and actually built houses on water. Yes, houses on water.

As you'll learn in the chapter that follows called *Water*, that's a walk in the park for the Dutch, the masters of making water bend to their will. The attraction of this form of accommodation is that you can stay in relative luxury somewhere that's right bang on the water with lovely views of canals, dykes, the whole Dutch shebang. If the sight of water makes you as giddy as it does me, then there's no finer place to call home during your time here. But sorry, this isn't about me. It's about finding you somewhere to stay. We'll assume that your choice of accommodation will be based on either price or location. The first we can't really help you with (sorry) but the second we certainly can. So without further ado, let's lead you through the parts of town where John would, and wouldn't, stay in Amsterdam.

THE JORDAAN

The Jordaan is one of those areas beloved of guidebooks and in-flight magazines that delight in telling you how 'hip' and generally wonderful it is here. And to be fair, it really is quite nice, being full of interesting shops and cafés tucked away in narrow lanes that are a pleasure to walk through. It's quite a turnaround for a neighbourhood that 100 years ago was the most over-populated slum in Europe, with over 150,000 people crammed into it. Today it's one of the most exclusive neighbourhoods in the Netherlands, with only 15,000 residents breathing its rarefied atmosphere.

The Jordaan is where the old, working class Amsterdam meets the new, flashy creative generation, a neighbourhood that on one hand has an annual festival based on the folk music that comes from the area (The Jordaan Festival, natch), and on the other is full of extravagant shops like Moooi, the boutique owned by Marcel Wanders, the legendarily flamboyant (and pretentious) Dutch designer. But in general it's the gentrified side of the Jordaan that dominates, making it the sort of area where the residents get bitchy if you speak a touch too loudly, thus disturbing the exclusive atmosphere they've paid an extortionate amount to preserve from the likes of you.

That aside, it is really quite a nice part of town. True, everything's on the expensive side, but as with every wealthy neighbourhood, there's a reason why people with money choose to spend it here. It's because the houses are old and attractive, the restaurants are good, the canals make everything extra pretty and there aren't (that) many tourists. Still, The Jordaan is comparatively down at heel compared to…

THE GRACHTENGORDEL

This is the epicentre of town, Amsterdam's canal district, that's made up of everything within Amsterdam's three and a half main canals: the Herengracht, Keizersgracht, Prinsengracht and Singel (that's the half one). It contains basically almost everything of historical interest (well, up to 1900 say) in the city and is undoubtedly the jewel in Amsterdam's crown, an area that has changed relatively little in the 400 years since it was first constructed. It's beautiful, picture postcard Amsterdam at its finest and was recently added to UNESCO's World Heritage list. Exhaustive scientific research has proven that it's so pretty that it's impossible to stroll around it without a smile on your face at all times.

However, this means that a house within its bounds is ridiculously expensive and that it's an area populated during the day by estate agents, bankers and advertising type people, and in the evening by estate agents, bankers and advertising people, except of a slightly older and even richer vintage. Despite the fact that its construction and the impact it had on Amsterdam's trade and prosperity are indirectly responsible for

Amsterdam's cultural diversity, it's almost exclusively inhabited by elderly white people, a feat of irony that's right up there with rain on your wedding day on the Morissette scale. As a temporary visitor to Amsterdam, however, this shouldn't put you off staying in the Canal District, since if you can score a hotel here, I'd hop on it like something that you want to hop on very much indeed, but just make sure you resist the temptation to stay within the Grachtengordel's bounds and head out to discover the rest of the city.

THE PIJP

The Pijp (it means, um, the pipe) is a neighbourhood just south of the Grachtengordel that was the original home of gentrification in Amsterdam and is probably one of the best places for you to stay in town. It's ideally located for almost everywhere you'd want to go elsewhere in the city, is a pretty nice neighbourhood and as it's not as cool as it used to be, so is a bit cheaper than it was a few years back. A bit like the Grachtengordel, you wouldn't want to spend all your time here, but as a base of operations, it's pretty much perfect.

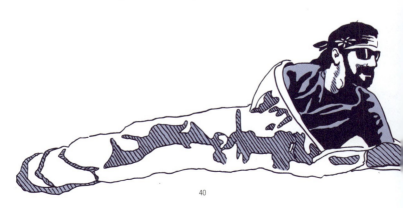

WEST IS HET BEST, OOST HEEFT THE MOST

Which roughly translated means West Amsterdam is the best, East Amsterdam has the most. A more poetic version of the two sides of the city's claims to superiority might have been West is the best, East is a beast, given that it rhymes and everything, but we like to be clear about things at The John Altman Organisation. What it really means is that East versus West is the only real rivalry in town. The North doesn't really count in most of Amsterdam's eyes, because you have to cross the river to get there, while the South is where the kind of people live who can't quite afford to live in the Grachtengordel or think it's too clichéd to do so. Either way, they don't concern themselves much with other people, so it's in East or West Amsterdam that most 'normal' people live.

It's quite hard to say that one is superior to the other, as both sides of the city are really quite similar in terms of attractions (cinemas, bars, restaurants, transport and proximity to the city centre) meaning that your preference will most likely lie where your friends or lovers live. True, both East and West Amsterdam are largely residential areas, but the law of economy dictates that as the rents are cheaper here, you get much more interesting people living and setting up shop here. In places like Studio K in East Amsterdam, an 'alternative' independent cinema/restaurant/concert venue that's always got something intriguing going on. Or OT301 on the Overtoom in West Amsterdam, another 'alternative' independent cinema/restaurant/concert venue that's always got something intriguing going on. I did say that East and West were quite similar…

Brouwerij 't IJ
A windmill, a canal and a glass of freshly brewed beer. It doesn't get much better in East Amsterdam.

To delve a little bit further into both areas, East Amsterdam is perhaps most famous for Artis Zoo - the most visited tourist attraction in Amsterdam, don't you know. The Indische Buurt is really nice, it's where the Dutch navy used to hang out. It's full of beautiful big old buildings and contains the Brouwerij 't IJ, somewhere you simply must visit. While at the end of the Czaar Peterstraat you've got Roest, a rather lovely bar set on a quayside, and the Dappermarkt and Zeeburg are the newer parts of town that are 'up and coming' in estate agent speak.

West Amsterdam, by which I mean anywhere west of the Prinsengracht, is also highly worthy of your investigation.

It boasts the Westerpark, the best park in Amsterdam, that contains a clutch of decent bars, restaurants and the Ketelhuis, one of the best cinemas in town. West has also got the Ten Katemarkt within its bounds (which is the best market in town), the best Turkish bakeries and in the form of the OT301 and the Nieuwe Anita two of the most interesting and individual places to go out at night. All of which is really rather splendid.

And that's Amsterdam in a nutshell. Really rather splendid. You're sure to find somewhere nice as almost every part of Amsterdam has something to recommend it and almost no part of Amsterdam is far enough away from the centre to discount it as a prospective place to stay. You're here (to stay) and that's the most important thing.

Which brings us back to where we started. *Oost, west, thuis best*. What it means is that it doesn't really matter whether you're in the East (*oost*) or the West (*west*), the best place to be is home (*thuis*). A sentiment that John would thoroughly approve of.

DOING NOTHING OUTSIDE
(That shows you how not to let the elements get in the way of doing nothing)

I originally intended to begin this chapter with a warning that doing nothing outside would be one of the hardest challenges you'd face during your time in Amsterdam. But in the grip of a slightly cynical mood swing (possibly induced by a bout of seasonal affective disorder), I came to the conclusion that it is, in fact, really, really easy. Because unless you happen to land upon these shores during the two weeks, or rather the fourteen days, scattered randomly between May and September that the calendar (if nobody else) calls summer, then you'll spend the vast majority of your time inside, looking forlornly at the rain tipping down outside. Or if you're daring enough to venture out of doors during the seemingly endless monsoon period that afflicts the city, rushing between one place and the other as fast as your legs or your bicycle pedals will carry you. And that's on the good days.

You might not have had John down as the sporty type (after all, it's a bit too much like doing something rather than nothing) but as long as it was about the taking part, rather than the winning, John was always up for a bit of fun and games. Especially a set or two of tennis and especially if it was mixed doubles. The way he wafted his racket gently back and forth disguised a fairly lethal forehand (that's no backhanded compliment).

Far from doing nothing, doing anything outside therefore becomes a question of whether you're going to let a spot of wind or rain get in the way of your holiday or not. Needless to say, John wouldn't. See, when looking for something to do outside, John's a typical Californian: he wants to be outdoors as much as possible, come rain or shine. Once there, all he's after is a nice place where he can make himself and his nearest and dearest comfortable with something to eat and drink, a nice

view to admire and the potential to share all of this with even more people. And if it were to rain? Well, either he'd grimace ever so slightly and put an umbrella up or just find something else to do. Fortunately for us all, the good people of Amsterdam are expert not only in the art of protecting themselves against the elements, but also at preparing themselves for every eventuality the weather can throw at them, be it sun, sleet or snow.

SINGING IN THE RAIN AND SKATING ON THIN ICE

As it isn't always sunshine, lollipops and rainbows in the Netherlands, Dutch society has come up with a vast array of ingenious ways to keep out the wind and rain. The daddy of this particular scene is the variety of all in one ponchos that keep not only your entire body dry, but your bike as well. The majority of wet weather gear designers are content to simply cover you from head to toe, but in Amsterdam you can go around town covered from head to toe and from front light to back light in the finest water resistant fabric known to mankind. Despite all appearances to the contrary (who isn't fond of a fetching anorak?), this isn't a fashion statement, but a simple matter of survival, a feat of design and engineering made even more impressive taking into account the considerable height and breath of the average Dutch adult, meaning that each poncho has to protect approximately 545m^3 of man and machine.

However, not even this latter-day miracle will help you in the time of the year that Amsterdam really shines, during the extremely cold winter snaps that normally occur between

December and March. With a mere dusting of snow Amsterdam turns into a veritable winter wonderland, but every so often it gets so cold that even the canals freeze. Then there's really no better time to see the city. To be fair, you might have little choice in the matter, as I did (or didn't) during the great snowpocalypse of 2009, the day when all of the Netherlands stopped, quite literally in its tracks.

Due to the immense snowfall (a whole two, maybe three, inches), there was no form of public transport available whatsoever. It was impossible to get anywhere unless you walked, and even that was made challenging by the hail of snowballs you had to endure whilst edging your way through the innumerable snowball fights that engulfed the city. If I hadn't missed my train to catch my boat home, I'd have loved it. In fact I still did. Why? Because, as in every time of trouble, I asked myself what would John do in this situation. The answer was that he'd embrace

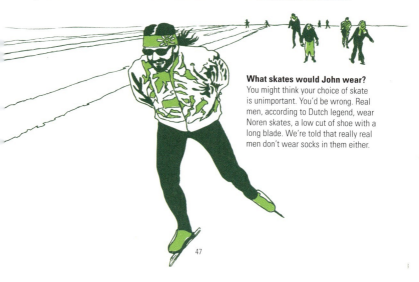

What skates would John wear?
You might think your choice of skate is unimportant. You'd be wrong. Real men, according to Dutch legend, wear Noren skates, a low cut of shoe with a long blade. We're told that really real men don't wear socks in them either.

the extra day in Amsterdam that he had been granted and take full advantage of the fact that it was impossible to do anything except act like you're five again and make the most of the snow. It's at times like this that the whole city stops and the skates can come out and Amsterdam becomes an official winter paradise. Skating is a serious business in Amsterdam, by the way. People actually watch it in pubs and everything. Yep, speed skating. That's the sport where two people in ridiculously tight and unflattering Lycra suits go round a track again and again and again. They don't even really overtake each other, just go round in circles waving their arms gently. And people say cricket's boring…

Fortunately doing it yourself is much more fun than watching it on TV. Every Dutch child is given a pair of skates as a coming of age present, and despite the fact that global warming means that the skates don't get taken out of the cupboard as often as they used to, as soon as there's a proper frost, the whole country's attention turns to the ice.
When it's thick enough, the canals fill with skaters eager to rediscover their skating skills. And of course, Amsterdam being Amsterdam and the Dutch being the Dutch, there'll also be some quick-witted entrepreneur there trying to make a quick buck or two by selling Erwtensoep (pea soup with bits of sausage thrown in) and mulled wine. It all makes for a veritable winter wonderland.

So that's what happens in winter/spring/autumn. Hopefully you can now appreciate why the people of Amsterdam go so crazy when the weather gets better. As soon as the sun comes out the whole city, bar none, empties onto the streets and occupies any and every piece of ground, water, or anywhere else that it's possible to park a posterior on while soaking up the sun. This is when doing nothing in Amsterdam reaches its apotheosis (I love that word, sorry).

TERRACES

The most basic, and simplest form of doing nothing in the sunshine is to indulge in the *terras* phenomenon. A *terras* is any piece of pavement outside a bar or any similar hostelry that undergoes a Cinderella style transformation when the sun comes out, as it turns from a humble piece of asphalt to the most desirable place to have a drink in town.

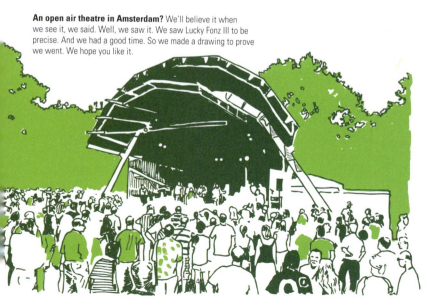

An open air theatre in Amsterdam? We'll believe it when we see it, we said. Well, we saw it. We saw Lucky Fonz III to be precise. And we had a good time. So we made a drawing to prove we went. We hope you like it.

To enjoy it like the locals is as easy as *een, twee, drie*, as essentially all it involves is sitting down and having a drink. All of which might not seem that remarkable to any foreign visitors, especially those from warmer climes, but for the Dutch, this is a moment to be seized, enjoyed and drawn out for as long as possible. Convention dictates that there are only two things that can be drunk in summertime – white beer for the gentleman and rosé wine for the ladies. Nothing else is acceptable, unless of course you choose to combine the two and drink rosé flavoured white beer (I kid you not, it really does exist).

There's only one barrier that separates you from some well-earned *terras* time and that's trying to find a seat in one. This is harder than it sounds, as they're snapped up faster than you can say "Ooh, look there's a couple of seats over there". If you are lucky enough to secure a spot, all that remains to do is to get your friends together and sit there until you've drunk enough to be unable to move anywhere else. It's as much fun as it sounds. But to take this to the next level, you need two things to really set the party off right. Food. And fire. Otherwise known as a barbecue.

BARBECUES

To barbecue *à la Hollandaise*, you only need three things – food, drink and a barbecue. As you probably won't be able to forecast with any degree of certainty the occasion on which you'll be allowed to get your grill out, you'll most likely have to assemble these tools as quickly as possible if you wish to barbecue. Which should be a pretty straightforward task, except for the fact that everyone else in the city has had exactly the same idea as you. Namely to go to the park and get drunk and eat food with their friends. So everybody, and I mean everybody, is already rushing to the supermarket to sort themselves out with some barbecuing gear.

The chances are that by the time you arrive at the supermarket, the shelves will most likely have already been stripped bare of anything that's vaguely barbecue related, be it wine, beer, crisps, or in fact anything edible or drinkable. And, of course, the magical, indispensable disposable barbecues themselves. So you'll have to be quick - or head to Blokker, a chain of hardware shops for your BBQ.

Now, all this might not sound very 'John', buying disposable goods, shopping in supermarkets, etc, but our hero is also a pragmatist. As he was fond of saying, he's 100% good, not perfect. It's the perfect get out of jail free card for almost any occasion - you should try it sometime. It means that he always tries his best to do his best for people and the planet, but sometimes, like when looking for a disposable barbecue, he falls short of moral or environmental perfection.

So if this one time you don't buy organic meat and throw a lot of stuff away, well, as long as you don't make a habit out of it and try and make up for it in the future,

that's okay. You tried. And you're on holiday, so you're alright in John's book (phew). If you really want to get into this Dutch style and make a proper occasion out of your day in the sun, you should also take some flags (practically obligatory if it's somebody's birthday) to deck the trees with, and maybe a football or ball game of some description to help you pass the time. To this end we've helpfully scattered a selection of games that John would play throughout these pages.

Getting back to the barbecue, time will fly by and the moment will arrive, around 10pm most likely, when it will get a little bit chilly, especially if you're doing this at the end or beginning of the BBQ season (in May and October respectively), and you may wish to choose to coax the gently glowing embers of the barbecue into something more resembling a campfire to keep the chill out of your bones. Strangely enough, this is something that the police and park authorities aren't that keen on. The line between a barbecue and a campfire is a fine one, but you can help yourself remain discreet by ensuring that the moment that you rock up with a huge amount of wood to throw on the fire doesn't coincide with the arrival of the representatives of law and order on the scene.

So remember John's golden rule, small is beautiful. And if you're caught red(wood) handed, just throw the incriminating evidence back into the bush where it came from. On one particularly memorable occasion a member of our party emerged with a log the size of a large canoe, a piece of wood so large and so obviously meant for burning that not even the most short-sighted policeman could have missed it or the intention for which it was meant. A Keystone Cops style chase ensued, but justice prevailed. Our man got away scot-free and we got to burn the log. It was a good day - and we didn't even have to use our AK.

Altman's Final Thought – in line with his 100% Good, Not Perfect philosophy, we'd like to ask you on John's behalf to make sure you clear up after yourself, recycle where possible and don't turn your fire into a forest fire. Thanks awfully.

WHERE TO PARK YOUR ARSE
Perhaps the most important detail for your BBQ is the location. As we mentioned in passing, your best bet is a park. But which park? If you ask most people, they'll direct you to the Vondelpark. You shouldn't listen to these people. Dismiss them immediately as frauds and charlatans as they clearly don't know what they're talking about. Why? Because they obviously haven't considered where John would go. And John, instead of settling for the Vondelpark would make his way to either

the Westerpark, Rembrandtpark, or Erasmuspark as they're all parks with real character, charm and good vibes.

To be fair to the Vondelpark, it's cited so often as the best by those people with a distinct lack of imagination as it's the biggest and relatively central. But these 'advantages' also tend to mean that it attracts pseudo-musicians playing guitars and bongos and those particularly annoying people on rollerblades who think it's cool to dash between plastic cups on the floor - plus the even more annoying people who think it's cool to watch.

All things considered, you'd be much better off going to the parks we mentioned earlier. Pretty much all of them are a little bit further out of the centre than the Vondelpark, but you'll be rewarded by seeing more of Amsterdam, geographically, physically and personally. And that's what we're here for after all.

The park that ticks the most John Altman boxes is the Westerpark. It's not too far from the centre and genuinely has something for everybody: bars, a cinema, tennis courts, an attractive pond, lots of grass and an overriding sense of industrial chic lent by the fact that the complex used to be a gasworks back in the day, the highlight of which is the gas holder itself. Every now and then there's a festival held in the park (Pitch is particularly good) and you get to go inside these wonderful buildings, and although the sound leaves a bit to be desired, the surroundings more than make up for it. The Westerpark is one of those rare places in a city where everyone gets down –

whether it's in the posh Westergas Terras restaurant, the arty cinema or just hanging out in the park - you'll see almost every slice of Amsterdam life represented here.

But the real magic of the Westerpark lies in the details, the little gems it's got tucked away like the wonderful children's farm all the way down the other end of the park (that sells really good beer really cheaply in its café) and the free tennis courts that are considerably easier to find than the farm. The tennis courts are run by Big Ali (this might not be his real name, but it's a good one), who is master of all he surveys in his realm, which amounts to the tennis courts, a café and some toilets, which you might find useful if you plan on spending an extended amount of time in the park. Everything he does is for free and everything he does is to provide a place for the local kids to play sport safely. The only price you have to pay for

Everyone in the world knows this wonderful sport as 'Boules' or 'Petanque,' apart from the Dutch who out of sheer bloody-mindedness call it 'Jeu de Boules'. Which, I would like to point out, although grammatically correct, is wrong. Anyway, there are a number of places to play it in Amsterdam, the best probably being in front of Café Hesp, by the Amstel. A proper gravel court with a river view and a decent bar a roll of the jacques away. Parfait!

his hospitality is that he might make some sort of joke about your appearance (although that seems to be par for the course with me in this country) as you dive into the loo. But that's a small price to pay for free tennis and toilets. Big Ali is, as John would say, a legend.

TAKING THE PISS
Finally, something for the gentlemen. One thing you might notice while strolling around Amsterdam are the public urinoirs. Then again, given the fact they're relatively discreet, you might not, although some might say that if the wind is blowing in the right direction and your nose is in full working order it's quite obvious what they're for. The single ones look a bit like an oil can with a grill on top, while the double ones, well, they look a bit like an oil can opened up with a grill on top.

You'll be pleased to hear that if you're a gentleman (or a particularly desperate lady) these quite brilliant public facilities entitle you to enjoy the privilege of peeing in the street. And they're free to use, so if you balk at paying the fifty cents that most clubs and bars charge you to go to the loo,

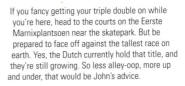

If you fancy getting your triple double on while you're here, head to the courts on the Eerste Marnixplantsoen near the skatepark. But be prepared to face off against the tallest race on earth. Yes, the Dutch currently hold that title, and they're still growing. So less alley-oop, more up and under, that would be John's advice.

The Dutch are really rather good at football. Annoyingly so. Before I came here, I used to fancy myself as a winger endowed with a set of skills and turn of pace that might not have been enough to trouble the professional ranks, but more than sufficient to be considered 'decent'. That was until I played with a Dutch team for the first time. It quickly disintegrated into a giant game of piggy in the middle as I chased the ball fruitlessly around the pitch while everyone pointed and laughed. Thankfully park football is a more relaxed affair, so don't hesitate to get involved.

these are the places for you. Helpfully they're relatively numerous and can be found regularly scattered through the city centre, so if you keep your eyes peeled, you'll never be caught short in Amsterdam again. The only downside is that you can't wash your hands afterwards. Still, it represents an opportunity to do something that's illegal in 23 states in America and using them remains a joy that never grows old.

Doing Nothing Inside

(That mainly concerns one of the hardest Dutch words to say that's not Scheveningen)

As readers of the preceding chapter will have noticed, Amsterdam is a city built on the premise that being indoors is better than outdoors. The positive to take out of this situation (looking on the bright side, if you will) is that it's ensured that the good people of Amsterdam excel at making it as pleasurable as possible for you to stay inside as long (and as comfortably) as the weather dictates.

Indeed, the Dutch love being indoors so much that they've even created a special word to describe the sensation of being blissfully happy indoors: *gezellig*.

It is, I'm afraid, rather a difficult word to pronounce, due to the unforgiving nature of the Dutch 'g,' but if you've been doing the homework prescribed for you at the start of the book, you

DOING NOTHING INSIDE

John au naturel
John getting in touch with nature during a flying visit to Artis Zoo.

should be ready to try it out by now. And if not, close your eyes, open your throat and let as much phlegm loose as you feel comfortable with, but remember to hold some back for the second 'g' at the end of the word. Don't worry if you can't get it out immediately, the power of the 'g' word to hit the right spot (the 'g' spot, you might say) should overcome any potential communication problems.

However, it is well worth persevering with your attempts to master its pronunciation, as *gezellig* is a word worth its weight in gold in Amsterdam, a word that's more a cultural phenomenon then a mere group of letters. As anyone who's spent more than five minutes in Amsterdam or around someone Dutch will tell you, *gezellig* is the stamp of quality for everything that's good in life.

The fact that the word itself is directly untranslatable is a source of great pride to the Dutch and gives them almost as much pleasure as *gezelligheid* (that's the noun, in case you were wondering) itself. The nearest equivalent we have in English is 'cosy' but that doesn't really do the full magnificence of the concept justice. John, as you may have learnt to expect by now, is the man who may have come closest to solving this mystery with his three magical words: 'spread the love!'

Because that's what *gezelligheid* is all about – doing something you enjoy with someone (or a group of people) you like, somewhere nice, warm and dry. Somewhere indoors, basically. So let's help you tap into the vibe forthwith.

WHERE TO FIND GEZELLIGHEID

The key to your finding the holy grail of *gezelligheid* lies within the time of day at which you'll be looking to wallow in Amsterdam's great indoors. Because although you may be looking to do nothing all day long, sadly the rest of the city isn't in the same enviable position. It may be stating the obvious to say that most of the city will be at work for most of the day, but it's of vital importance that you take this fact on board as despite your status as a tourist the rhythm of your day in Amsterdam will be dictated, or strongly influenced at the very least, by the Dutch working day.

Why? Because the Dutch adhere rather rigidly to the 9-5 working regime. They arrive work at 9am precisely, they leave at 5pm on the dot (or on the nose as they say here). Not because they're strictly business (EPMD, salute!) but they have the common sense to value their personal lives as much as their career. People here work hard then go home to make the most out of their personal life as well, a state of affairs that

Bitterballen
The 'brown fruit' of the brown café, a bitterbal is piping hot (and we mean HOT) meat encased in a thick breadcrumb crust and best enjoyed dipped in mustard. If you don't want to endure first-degree burns on the inside of your mouth, let them cool for a good ten minutes before consuming.

must be applauded. It makes you wonder why we don't all do it. However you may feel slightly differently about it when you're confronted with a 'closed' sign at a minute past six and thus faced with the prospect of facing your host for the evening without a present for them or telling your other half that you couldn't pick up some nappies for your child so baby will just have to turn her nappy inside-out this evening. Yes, that's because the 9-5 philosophy applies not only to office hours but to each and every hive of industry in the city: shops, hairdressers, museums, bakeries, tinkers, tailors, soldiers and spies all close their doors to business at 5pm precisely. To be fair, Amsterdam is considerably more liberal than the rest of the Netherlands in this respect; the shops here are open until 6pm, sometimes until 7pm and sometimes even on Sundays!

The only exceptions to the rule are the ubiquitous Albert Heijn supermarkets that remain open all the way through from 8am until 10pm, but you don't really want to shop there. They're generally over-priced and under-stocked, and there's little to recommend them apart from a lovely anecdote from Danny Wallace's excellent book *Yes Man*. The premise of the book is that Danny has to say yes to everything, including an email from a Nigerian banker asking him if he'd like to make lots of money. To cut a long story short, Danny is given a name in Amsterdam to contact for his million pounds, a certain Albert Heijn. It turns out that the address Danny has been given for Mr. Heijn is false, but remarkably the first person he turns to in the street knows where Albert Heijn lives! Even better, he can be found just around the corner! A turn of events that delights Danny until he arrives at the local supermarket bearing the name of his contact. Chortle. Anyway, you should really read the whole book, it's pretty good, as is Danny's other book about starting a cult (The Karma Army) called *Join Me*.

But to return to the matter in hand, Amsterdam's restricted opening hours would most certainly meet with John's approval as they place an unofficial emphasis on things that aren't any form of regulated activity like working or shopping. Past 7pm you simply can't do much but go home or go out. Either way you'll be enjoying yourself and spending quality time with people you love. Or as it's otherwise known, doing nothing. Hooray! So to help you get the most out of Amsterdam's great indoors, we'll show you how John himself would do it.

John's coffee of choice in Amsterdam would be a koffie verkeerd. The name means 'inverted coffee' as usually a coffee is lots of coffee and a little milk, but in a 'verkeerd' it's the other way round. It's so wrong, it's right.

DOING NOTHING INSIDE DURING THE DAY

John was never a man given to rising early, especially on holiday. Thus it's fair to say that he wouldn't expect you to get up at the crack of dawn either. Besides, beds and Amsterdam always held a special place in his heart after that other famous John's bed-in with Yoko back in the day at the Amsterdam Hilton. Our John would never confirm or deny his presence at this event, but if you look closely at the pictures, you can't help but notice a man with a beard and a flower in his hair grinning rather broadly. We'll say no more.

In fact, there was only one thing that would force John from his bed and that was his chronic need to get his early morning coffee fix. Nothing would do but a proper cup of coffee, freshly brewed - with plenty of milk and one and half sugars, in case you're wondering. Fortunately Amsterdam is blessed with plenty of places to find a good one of these as the Dutch take their coffee seriously. They make it with real beans in top of the range Italian machines and everything. It's what you'd expect really from a city that was the largest European importer of coffee back in the day.

Upon settling on somewhere to sup his first caffeine hit of the morning, John would make himself comfortable, nibble a pastry perhaps, shoot the breeze with whoever would listen, peruse that morning's The Guardian, Pitchfork and The Onion online (almost every café in Amsterdam has free Wi-Fi), have another cup of coffee, accompanied by a slice of cake this time perhaps (apple pie's a Dutch favourite), and consider what to do next. Where would John go to do this? Well, any place with the word *Koffie* emblazoned on the windows that looks appealing and is well stocked with board games or other suitable ways of passing the time. John was always fond of places where you can combine culture and coffee. Like the Mozaïek in West Amsterdam, a theatre/cultural centre in the heart of Bos and Lommer with an excellent café and a sun drenched terrace in the summer. There are exhibitions, plays and concerts on all the time here, so if so inclined you could easily pass the whole day here without any difficulty.

Or if you're looking to impress someone, head to De Balie. This is the honourable exception to the rule that everything on the Leidseplein should be given as wide a berth as possible. It's another sort of cultural centre that offers exhibitions, plays and, yes a café for your consideration, but as it's slap bang in the centre of town it serves mainly as a place where 'creative' people come to meet and show everyone just how creative they are by getting their MacBooks out and talking loudly about their latest schemes for world domination. So if you can ignore them or find this atmosphere invigorating, come on in. The food is decent, the beer selection excellent and it's nice and light thanks to the high windows.

Once his morning coffee craving had been satisfied, John would normally go and stretch his legs, perhaps to investigate one of Amsterdam's many forms of cultural stimuli. There's a thriving arts scene here and more museums per square metre than anywhere else in Europe - that's what I call a good fact. And the way that John went round museums ensured that it could never turn into a drag.

Upon entering a museum, he wouldn't head for a specific piece, but would dash through the museum as quickly as possible, clocking the exhibits that he deemed worthy of another look on the second round. Upon his return to the galleries (after a quick break in the café for further reflection) John would give every painting that had piqued his interest the full attention he felt it deserved. And if nothing he'd seen was up to scratch, why, he'd just walk straight out.

However, given that you have to shell out quite a consisum to enter every museum in Amsterdam you might have to be a touch more circumspect in selecting which one you wish to grace with your presence. Everyone knows about the Rijksmusuem and the Van Gogh, but we'd like to direct you to Foam, a photography museum on the Keizersgracht. There's always something interesting on there, presented without any form of pretension, the location is a picture (sorry) and the café in the basement is excellent, which is a pleasant bonus.

Another museum that would take John's fancy John is the Stedelijk Museum. For the last couple of years it's been without a fixed home and thus has popped up in a couple of locations around town for a couple of months before disappearing again. The idea of a vanishing museum appealed greatly to John, not least because the chance was great that he had a legitimate excuse for not visiting it and therefore for doing nothing. But on the off chance that it was open, after he'd finished there it would probably be five o'clock, otherwise known in the Altman household as beer or drink o'clock.

However if there was time before beer o'clock, there might just be time for a quick spot of shopping to pick up a pair of clogs, some tulips, a Rembrandt or other essential Amsterdam souvenirs. But on the whole shopping's not really a John Altman thing to do. Not because John's violently anti-consumerist, but more because it comes down on the 'doing something' side of the scales. Of course, if you fancy doing a spot of window shopping, we're not going to stop you, but we'd hope that on the way you'd get waylaid by a much more pleasurable place to spend your time and your Euros. Welcome to the heart of Amsterdam after-hours culture: the brown café.

DOING NOTHING AFTER HOURS

The first time I ventured inside a brown café was by accident. I didn't know Amsterdam very well, I had no idea what a brown café was, and I was trying to take a couple of friends to check out the Pijp, as I'd heard it was cool - an idea that tells you just how little I knew Amsterdam back then. In short, it was an expedition doomed to failure.

Paradiso. Probably the best place to see a concert in the world.

We got off on the wrong foot by getting on the wrong tram and ended up in the middle of nowhere - or as close to the middle of nowhere as it's possible to get in Amsterdam. As we neared the end of the line we decided to cut our losses, get off and retrace our steps. The female half of our trio (her opinion counted for so much that her stake in our trio rose immediately from a third to a half, if not two halves) was distinctly unimpressed with everything – the lack of direction, the amount of walking we were doing, my apparent lack of concern at the gravity of the situation, the pressure on her bladder - so as an immediate solution to all of these problems we popped in for a drink at the nearest hostelry. A bar with a welcoming neon light proudly proclaiming the legend: Café Riviera. You can't go wrong with a name like that, I thought. Karen, for that was her name, thought differently. Five years on, she still maintains it's the worst bar she's been to in the world. And she was brought up in Essex.

But even though the beer in Café Riviera was no better than passable, the music was of dubious quality and the level of body odour disturbingly high, there was something appealing about the place. I mean there was beer, the woman behind the bar was über-friendly and we had enough time to play a quick game of darts while Karen was in the loo. You see, what Karen missed was that what makes brown cafes so special is their status as authentic Amsterdam institutions. They're places where only people from Amsterdam hang out. And there's nowhere else but Amsterdam that you'll find bars like this, which is as good a reason as any to venture inside.

If you follow John down this proverbial rabbit hole, as you enter you'll be struck by the unmistakable aroma of *frituurvet* (aka the fumes from a deep fat fryer that hasn't been changed for fifteen years) stale beer and cigarettes. A heady combination, I'm sure you'll agree. And yes, you read cigarettes correctly. Because although it's been illegal in The Netherlands to smoke indoors for a few years, in brown cafés they flout this law with impunity. Quite possibly because it represents an integral part of their heritage, as the reason they got their name comes from the years of tobacco smoke that stained the walls (tobacco) brown. But what really makes brown cafés worth a look is because they're the best place to experience proper Dutch music. Well, maybe not proper Dutch music, but popular Dutch music.

Dutch pop music is a thriving industry that seems to flourish irrespective of fashion, trend or time. Dutch *volksliedjes* (that's the name of the genre in case you wish to make a request) can be broadly divided into two categories – happy songs and sad songs. A happy song is fast, ridiculously cheerful and has a big chorus with lots of 'la la las' that you can spot coming a mile off. The desired effect is that everyone in the audience should start waving their hands around in the air like they're changing a light bulb, or form a conga line (while still waving their hands around in the air).

A sad song is basically the same but a bit slower, with a more melancholy melody and an equally big chorus. What we're after in this category are tears, pure and simple, and lots of them. This sort of song is delivered sitting on a stool with lots of fist clenching and closed eyes during the choruses allowing plenty of opportunity for the singer to show us how much they're hurting deep inside. Both types of song are generally performed by people who take their style cues from either Liberace or Garth Brooks and their stage antics from *X Factor*. It's not pretty but it can be a lot of fun, at least for the first five minutes. But don't worry; there is other, better music to be found in Amsterdam in abundance, just not in the brown cafes. So if, like Karen, you don't feel that all the above represents a respectable form of entertainment for the evening, then you should avail yourself of one of the more reputable musical venues that Amsterdam has to offer.

Many of the world's greatest artists stop off in Amsterdam (who isn't interested in a break in the Dam?) and can be seen on a much more intimate scale than in London or New York. And for some reason the crowds here are always much more up for having a good time than in other capital cities – credit the Dutch enthusiasm for foreign performers, the *joie de vivre* that floods through the city, or the high spirits inspired in performers by the canals, or coffeeshops, of Amsterdam, whatever it is, it works. And if it's good enough for Keith Richards (who cited the Paradiso as one of his favourite places to play in his otherwise forgettable autobiography), it's good enough for John.

Most 'big' or up and coming acts will play either the Melkweg or the Paradiso. Both host about 1500 people in the main rooms and a couple of hundred in the small rooms, and both are excellent venues to see a concert. And both will charge you *lidmaatschap* - membership - on top of your ticket. It's 3.50 at Paradiso and 4 at Melkweg and you have to pay it to get in. I'm not sure why, probably something to do with fleecing you a little bit more, but you do have to pay it, sorry. On the plus side your membership does last for a month and the toilets here are free.

Huge artists, the kind of inexplicably popular acts like Kasabian and Katie Melua, will play the Heineken Music Hall, but you should steer well clear of this place. It may proudly proclaim that it has the best acoustics in Europe, but in reality it's a huge aircraft hanger of a venue with no soul that comes as close to packaging a music experience it's possible to get. If you're into classical music, it's the Concertgebouw you're after, jazz in the Bimhuis, hip hop and soul nights in Bitterzoet (or the Duivel, but at the time of going to press it was shut for three months after a shooting there, so who knows what's going to happen).

Electronic music you'll find all over the place, Trouw and Club Up being the current flavour of the month when we last checked, and if you want something completely different, try the OT301 and De Nieuwe Anita. All of them have websites, most of them in English, so just type the name into Google or stick .nl at the end and you should find them. And if you'd like to pick up some of the music you've heard in a brown café, or just fancy a spot of crate digging, head to Distortion Records.

It's on the Westerstraat in the Jordaan, sells mainly vinyl (John's weapon of choice for music) and has everything from rock and roll to dubstep in stock. And we're reliably informed that you can smoke inside if you so desire. You might even bump into Amsterdam's finest DJ $jammie the Money pulling records down from the stacks in there.

So that, by and large, is how John would make the most of a day inside doing nothing. As brown cafes are generally open as late as the owner wishes, it's an itinerary that should keep you going for a good while. As a last tip, we'll leave you with the information that the Dutch for after-party is *afterparty*. Enjoy.

Fietsen
(Or how my mum learned to stop worrying and love the bike)

When I was 6 I fell off my bike and cracked my head open. I'd just mastered the art of how to ride a bike (or to be strictly accurate, how to stay on it for longer than five seconds) and had decided that I wanted to emulate the big boys in the park on their BMXs and pull some sick tricks of my own. Sadly neither my skills nor my brand new Snoopy Chopper (complete with streamers and Snoopy nose horn) were up to the task and instead of doing a 360 I landed straight on my head. I spent the next two days in hospital and my mum spent the next twenty years worrying incessantly every time I left the house on two wheels. So when she heard that I was going to live in Amsterdam and that my principal form of transportation was going to be the bicycle, well, she came closer to flipping than I did all those years ago in Barnard Park. No matter how much I assured her that cycling in Amsterdam was as easy as falling off a log (not the best choice of metaphor perhaps) she refused to believe me when I told her that Amsterdam, aka the bike capital of world, is indeed the safest and bestest place to ride your bicycle in the known universe. However, when she actually came here for the first time and saw the multitude of bike lanes and just how easy and pleasant it is to cycle here, she was happy. So just in case you had any doubts about cycling here, it is now officially a mum approved activity, a level of accreditation that really seals the deal on why the humble bicycle is the only way that John would go around town in Amsterdam. It's good for the environment. It's good for you. It's fun. And it doesn't get any better than that.

Cycling may not be obligatory in Amsterdam (yet), but it might as well be. People just look at you in bewilderment if you're on two feet rather than two wheels. Having said

What would John ride?
The easiest thing to pick up in Amsterdam is a hire bike. Because, well, it's the practical thing to do. You may not be here for long, and if you rent a bike you don't have to worry about losing it, insurance or a multitude of other things. But in case you're tempted into a more long-term relationship with a bike, we've put together a list of the most common bikes you'll see in town, with the best being awarded a What Would John Ride (WWJR) rating.

The Burco
Named after the old Amsterdam bike factory that first churned out this model a long, long time ago - in the good old days, some might say. It's the perfect choice for any respectable gentleman about town.

WWJR tip #1 (for the gents)

that, it is actually worth walking around for a bit to experience the disdain you'll have heaped on you for daring to forsake the bicycle and then to luxuriate in the resultant pride engendered by mounting one for the first time and circulating around Amsterdam in the manner in which it should be done. You'll go from zero to hero in five seconds.

Once on your bike, you'll soon discover that cycling in Amsterdam is nothing less than an absolute joy. Five years after I first started cycling here, it's still my favourite thing about living here. And conveniently it also fits in rather nicely with the concept of doing nothing.

Okay, cycling does inherently involve moving your legs back and forth, up and down, in a smooth circular fashion hundreds,

The Omafiets.
Otherwise known as 'the granny bike' because its frame makes it super easy for ladies (and gentlemen) of the less flexible kind to get on and off this hugely aesthetically pleasing machine. WWJR tip #1 (for the ladies).

if not thousands of times. Depending on your level of enthusiasm, it might even involve strenuous effort at one point or another. But don't worry about it, cycling in Amsterdam really is very easy. You only have to clock how many people of ample girth there are in the city who cycle regularly to see that it's not exactly a fitness sport. Much after the Victorian fashion, breaking into a sweat whilst cycling is positively not encouraged here. Indeed it's almost impossible to achieve unless it's the height of summer and you're carting about six suitcases around town. Which, as a potential visitor to this fair city on a summer holiday, isn't that far-fetched a scenario. Although given the weather Amsterdam has been blessed with between May and August in recent years, you might not have to worry about this so much.

TWO WHEELS GOOD, FOUR WHEELS BAD

What makes a bicycle so valuable in Amsterdam is that it represents your pass to the freedom of the city; the ability to travel wherever you want, whenever you want. And it gets

Kinderbakfiets
Put your children in the front, a look of carefree nonchalance on your face and a string of pearls around your neck and you're ready to mount the ultimate accessory for yummy mummies.

even better: as we've said, Amsterdam's a small city, so with a bike the whole city becomes instantly accessible with even the extremities of east and west Amsterdam only a half hour cycle ride apart. And even better, because Holland's a small country, it's not too far-fetched to say that you could keep on cycling out of Amsterdam and have a look around a nearby village, get off to smell the tulips and be back home in time for tea.

Having a bike also means that you'll be independent of public transport, meaning no waiting at bus stops (a bad way of doing nothing), no standing on crowded trams with your face in someone's armpit and no buses, full stop. Not that public transport is particularly bad, or expensive, it's just a bit underwhelming. Not particularly clean, not particularly dirty, not particularly exciting, no great views, nothing chaotic, just well, not much to write home about. Whereas you can fill a whole chapter of a book on the humble bicycle. Need we say more? Well, yes, we probably should given that we've just started a chapter on that very subject. But seriously, cycling in Am-

The Bakfiets
Unlike the kinderbakfiets, the true form of the bakfiets is really rather cool. It's huge, decidedly unwieldy, has a handle for a break, can't go very fast, and is thus excellent for holding up traffic - and moving house. WWJR tip #2.

sterdam is easy peasy. You can't get lost, and if you do, there's always a distraction *en route* worth stopping off at for a quick break. All you need to get started is a bike, so let's introduce you to what will become your bosom buddy in Amsterdam.

MOUNTING YOUR FAITHFUL STEED

When you first get on a Dutch bike you might be a bit confused. Not only by the apparent lack of brakes but also the distinct lack of gears. But fret not, you haven't been ripped off or handed a dodgy bike, just a Dutch bike. Which you'll soon learn (if you haven't guessed already) is the very best in the world.

Gears? For pussies. You'll have no need of them here. Brakes? Ha. A luxury. Why burden a bike frame with brakes when pedalling backwards will do the job equally as well? This form of braking has the added attraction of making a 'routine' stop doubly exciting in the rain, as you can never really predict how long your braking distance will be. Backwards is the new forwards, you know?

The Racer
The first bike I ever had was a racer bike. Actually, it was a chopper. The first bike I ever bought was a racer - a rare thing of beauty it was too. Sadly it's not really a bike that thrives in Amsterdam, a cycling environment that favours stability over speed and delicacy. But if you're brave enough to hop on it, John would certainly approve.

But the most important addition to a Dutch bike is what you'll find above the back wheel. It might look like a run of the mill bike rack for putting your shopping on that you'd find anywhere in the world, but in Amsterdam, it transforms into a passenger seat for your bike. Ingenious! And practical too. As you'll learn, the bicycle in Amsterdam isn't merely THE mode of transport but a way of life. A philosophy if you will.
It's almost Buddhist in its application: you get out of it what you put in. And the Dutch put a lot into (and onto) the bike. The basic rule is that if you can carry it in your arms, you can carry it on a bike, be it a shopping bag, ghettoblaster or chest of drawers. Or a person, which brings us back to the newfound passenger seat on the back of your bike. You can put anything and anyone on your bike - within reason, one passenger is more than enough.

Although if your passenger is of a somewhat larger disposition, you should ask them politely to mount your bike with caution,

The 'Fixie'
If you've read any magazine vaguely fixated with the concept of 'cool' in the last ten years, you'll probably be aware that the fixed gear bike is, indeed, 'cool.' At least it was 10 years ago. Sadly it's now become the preserve of ageing graphic designers clinging desperately to any last vestige of cool they can grab. Still, you've got a couple of years until accountants lay their hands on them, so if you want to try a 'fixie' out, you can still do so without losing too much dignity. Although any vestige of self-respect will disappear as soon as you try to ride one of the confoundedly impractical things.

otherwise your bike might not take too kindly to them. Even a Dutch bike has its limits. A bent wheel is easier to fix than you may imagine, but wheeling it through town while everyone points and laughs is much harder. If you're not feeling confident enough to try making a bicycle made for one into one made for two, just sit back and watch the Dutch do what they do best. Ride bikes.

A FEW GROUND RULES

It's probably worth giving you a few pointers to the rules of the road, I mean, the cycle path. After all, this is the country where the highest compliment you can be paid is: "Will, you know, for a foreigner, you're really quite good at riding a bike." This is a country that thinks they invented the bike and bicycle culture, when all they really did was have the good fortune to be the flattest country on earth.

Van Moof
This is the new generation of Amsterdam bike - the Burco for the 21st century if you will. Its design divides opinion, but if you want a modern take on the genuine Amsterdam bike, Van Moof is the place to be.

Still, this doesn't stop them from proudly (and frequently) proclaiming that they're the best people in the world at riding bikes. There may not be many recent Dutch winners of the Tour de France, but they do spend a staggering amount of time on a bike. Some Dutch people are so attached to their bikes that they even take them into the bedroom. Seriously, I've seen it. Disturbingly, I've also done it myself a couple of times.

You might think you're an accomplished cyclist if you can take your hands off the handlebars for ten seconds while moving, but in Amsterdam that's child's play. Here they do it while rolling a cigarette, reading a book and talking on the phone - all at the same time.

However, the good news for mothers everywhere is that you should find it virtually impossible to have an accident on your bike. There are bicycle lanes everywhere. Indeed no street is

BMX
If you pull sick tricks, yes. If you physically recoil at reading those words, no.

complete without one thanks to the efforts of the Dutch government in the 70s, and if you ever find yourself off one and in the middle of the road you're probably doing something wrong - and you'll soon hear about it from a car or other road user.

The first rule of the road in Amsterdam is to watch out for tramlines. And by watch out, I mean don't stick your wheel in them. Like I did once while trying to overtake someone. It ended rather nastily, mainly because as I was falling relentlessly towards the ground on my left hand side, I realised that my iPod was in the left hand pocket of my jeans. So to preserve it, I summoned up the desperate strength that comes only when faced with the very worst kinds of catastrophe, wrenched the steel bike over (it must have weighed about 1000 kilos), and fell not so gently onto the other side of my body. Happily my iPod emerged from this monument to hubris unscathed, the right side of my body slightly less so.

The rest of my journey home proceeded relatively smoothly, although it did feel like everybody was looking at me rather

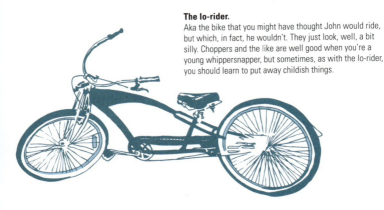

The lo-rider.
Aka the bike that you might have thought John would ride, but which, in fact, he wouldn't. They just look, well, a bit silly. Choppers and the like are well good when you're a young whippersnapper, but sometimes, as with the lo-rider, you should learn to put away childish things.

strangely. I assumed it was just because the Dutch could instinctively tell that I'd had an accident on a bike and were thus deeply ashamed on my behalf. When I got home I realised it was more to do with the fact that my face was covered in blood. Still, at least I'd had the soothing sounds of Jorge Ben's *A Tábua de Esmeralda* to comfort me on the journey home - and in the three years since that my iPod and I have been together. Win some, lose some.

Anyway, so long as you steer clear of the tramlines you'll be okay. A general rule of thumb is that if you're able to get on your bike, then you're okay to ride it. Unlike the time that a friend of mine had had one drink too many and when he tried to mount his faithful steed to go home, fell over the frame twice before shamefacedly walking away.

The other good thing about being on a bike is that you won't piss off Dutch people when you mistakenly wander into the

The Fietstaxi
You'll see a lot out of these about town. The simplest way to convey to you how much of a plague on society they are would be to say that if you step inside one, you're dead to John. And to us. Sorry, that's just the way it is. They're a handcart to hell - they take all the space in the cycle lanes, they go infuriatingly slowly and they smell. Rant over.

cycle lane. It's an easy trap to fall into, as for the uninformed, a cycle lane does look just like any other piece of asphalt. But no. As soon as you walk onto the cycle lane you're walking onto a piece of turf as hallowed as any religious site in the world, as a cacophony of bicycle bells (the single most annoying sound in the known world) will immediately tell you - followed by someone speeding past and saying something derogatory about your mother. So make sure to give the cycle path a wide berth at those moments that you're not on a bike.

And that's about it. If you follow the rules we've set and use a little common sense, the most challenging obstacle you should face is climbing one of the bridges lining the canals.

NOT SO FINE
The only problem with having a country that's made for bicycles is that they're also subject to rather more stringent regulations than in the rest of the world. Like, they actually

The Fietsenmaker

Your bike's best friend in Amsterdam is the fietsenmaker – the bike shop. And as your bike is your best friend in Amsterdam, that makes the fietsenmaker a very important chap indeed. He can mend punctures, put your chain back on, straighten a bent wheel or any other problem that you may have with your bike. And he'll do all this with a smile, wink and without condescension – which is particularly useful when you come in with a particularly stupid problem. If you're really lucky, he'll show you how to do it as well.

And the best thing is that if you've got a flat tyre, you can just use the pump outside for free. Bonus.

enforce the law that you have to have front and tail headlights on your bike when it's dark. If you don't, you'll be fined. Rather heavily. And you have to wait at a red light. As if you cross cycle through one, you'll be fined. Rather heavily.

If you insist on flouting the law, the best tip we'd give you is that you spot the police and climb off your bicycle before they see you: it's perfectly legal to walk with a bike with no lights on the street, just not ride it. So hop off in time, look suitably nonchalant and wait a suitable interval before getting back on and you should get away with it.

You will of course need to ensure you do this unobserved, rather than making eye contact with the policeman as you slide off the bike and trying to style it out, claiming you've been walking it all the time. It's also not advised when the policeman says "Are you suggesting I'm blind?" to reply "Well, you are wearing glasses" as you'll most likely be invited to sample the delights of an Amsterdam cell for the evening or add another couple of zeroes to your fine.

THE CITY ON LOCKDOWN

Once you've got your hands on a bike (or your feet on the pedals, whichever way you want to look at it) you'll want to keep hold of it. Which sounds simple, but it isn't, since the only thing the Dutch love more than riding bikes is stealing bikes. To be honest, this shouldn't be a problem that you should be confronted with, as if you hire a bike from somewhere like MacBike, you can take it for granted that it'll be painted gaudily and come with an impregnable lock or two, a combination that should ensure that no one will steal it. Which is good. However, the considerable downside of a hire bike is that it marks you out immediately as a tourist and therefore not Dutch and therefore an inferior cyclist. It doesn't matter if you're Eddie Merckx or Mark Cavendish, if you ain't Dutch, you ain't much on a bike, so be prepared to be greeted with a series of sighs and frowns when people clock you as a non-Amsterdammer.

However, like I said, the silver lining to this particular cloud is that people won't nick your bike and that means that hopefully you'll never have to endure the pain of having a bike stolen. It happened to me three times in the first six weeks I was in The Netherlands, and it didn't get any easier the more it happened. The first time was particularly bad. I had just been given a shiny new *omafiets* and every morning I would wake, draw the curtains and look down adoringly at my new ride and sigh in happy contentment. Until one morning when I opened the curtains to see that my bike wasn't there. I knew it should be, as I'd locked it securely it to the bike stand. Still, I ran downstairs in my dressing gown (PG Wodehouse eat your heart out) to check. Sadly my eyes hadn't deceived me. My bike was gone and there was no trace of its departure. As I walked upstairs I tried to formulate a possible explanation for this tragic turn of events, eventually arriving at the only possible scenario: that someone's child had been taken seriously ill in the middle of the night and that their own bike had got a puncture, so they had been impelled to take mine to ensure their child didn't die. This was of course fine with me (it's all about spreading the love, you know?) as I knew that the happy ending to this story would entail my bike being returned to me later that afternoon with a note explaining everything and a bunch of flowers to apologise for the inconvenience.

Sadly neither the note, the flowers nor the bike were forthcoming. I did however spend the next couple of years scouring the streets for a blue omafiets and once accosted a twelve-year-old kid riding a bike suspiciously like mine, but after his mother and the police intervened, I accepted that perhaps it wasn't mine after all.

Moral of the story – tie your bike up securely with at least five locks and don't make any accusations that can't be backed up in court.

WHERE WOULD JOHN GO?

Water

(That's where it's at in Amsterdam)

Wherever you go in Amsterdam, there's no escaping the water. In the canals, in the rain, in the river, in the sea, water is everywhere in generous quantities. But before you start having second thoughts about getting on that 'Dam plane, you should know that this abundance of water is most definitely a Good Thing. For if there's one place where people know how to deal with water, it's the Netherlands. The Dutch know water and how to manage it like nobody else; after all, they raised half their country out of it. Sadly they haven't quite worked out how to make wine out of water yet (just beer) but the tap water in Amsterdam really is some of the best in the world. It's all to do with the sand dunes outside the city near Zandvoort apparently... You see, Amsterdam is a city made and defined by water. By the way,

this is one of the rare sentences in this book that can be backed up with cold, hard facts - water constitutes 10% of the surface area of the city fact fans, 20 km^2 out of 200km^2. And if you'd like another fun fact (who wouldn't?) then try this for size – Amsterdam itself is below sea level. As is Schiphol Airport. So if and when the floods come, it'll get interesting to say the least.

In fact it wouldn't be a complete over exaggeration to claim that Amsterdam owes both its very existence and prosperity to humble H2O. Amsterdam first rose to prominence in the 13th century when it served as the main point for importing Belgian beer into the Netherlands, and when the Dutch East

The Houseboat
If there was any doubt remaining about the houseboat's status as the pre-eminent form of boat in Amsterdam, allow us to present you with the Poezenboot: a shelter for homeless and abused cats in Amsterdam, that is, you guessed it, on a houseboat. Sweet.

India Company ruled the waves during the country's Golden Age, guess where all the loot from the new world was stockpiled? And it was during the Golden Age (apologies for the brief history lesson) that the Grachtengordel, you know, the Canal District we talked about earlier, was constructed. And it was the construction of the Grachtengordel that is largely responsible for how Amsterdam looks and acts today.

Looks, because the four principle canals of the Grachtengordel, together with the natural boundaries imposed by the river Ij, make it virtually impossible for the city to expand beyond its current size. So the Grachtengordel looks pretty much exactly the same as it did 400 years ago. Well, maybe 200 years ago. Amsterdam's timeless appearance is also supported, almost quite literally, by the wooden poles embedded in the marshy sand beneath the city (at depths of 13 and 18 metres no less)

The Sloep

63.8% of the boats you'll see afloat on Amsterdam's canals will be sloeps. What they perhaps lack in beauty, they more than make up for in practicality, a triumph of form over function. Strangely, unlike bicycles, people round here don't tend to steal boats, probably because they go so slowly that the chance of making a quick, and therefore successful, getaway is approximately zero.

that prop the city up. The city centre, at least on the right side of the river Ij, thus remains unmolested by skyscrapers or any other form of modern architecture. This has preserved the unique charms of the Grachtengordel forever, even if the centre's picture perfect status does give rise to questions like the one I heard from one American visitor: "What time does this place shut?" No, not the bar we were in, but Amsterdam itself, as if the entire city were some sort of Euro Disney amusement park built for their amusement.

It's an illusion that's particularly seductive when ensconced on a boat cruising along Amsterdam's canals. The whole experience, the atmosphere, the architecture, the waves lapping at the sides of the boat and the overriding feel of decadence all feel just a bit too good to be true.

The Canoe
Despite the placid nature of Amsterdam's waters, canoeing assumes a slightly extreme nature here due to the hazards involved in picking your way between the various forms of motorboat too busy enjoying themselves to notice a humble canoe. Though they might notice a foghorn, savvy?

But true it is and the influence of water in Amsterdam runs far deeper than buildings, through the very character of the city in fact. Because of the geographical and topographical restrictions the canal district places on the city, the people who live within its bounds have always had to live on top of each other and therefore accept each other because, well, they have to. If you live so close to one another there's simply no other option but to get on with your neighbours. Combine this with the traditionally high level of immigration that you find in a port, the hordes of sailors and traders that used to drop in from all over the globe and the reasons for Amsterdam's legendary melting pot liberality (and the Red Light District) begin to swim into focus.

And the reason for Amsterdam's status as a capital of creativity too. Amsterdam, as you may or may not be aware, is a highly creative city (at least it likes to cultivate that impression), famed for producing, or giving a home to painters, designers, illustrators, architects and other assorted creative types. You'll bump into so many artistic people here that you could be forgiven for thinking that all this creativity is stimulated by something in the water - and I hope you'd forgive me for saying it. But really and truly it must be something to do with the canals. I mean, everything else is. But you don't have to take my word for it. The positive effects of water in stimulating creativity are well documented and substantiated by no less an authority than Bruce Lee. Actor, legend and good friend to John Altman.

John did the catering for *Enter The Dragon* and between takes Brucey and John would chew the fat on subjects varying from the 49ers' prospects for the Super Bowl to the merits of Confucianism over Taoism. When the conversation veered round to Amsterdam, where Bruce was due to film *Chinese Kung Fu Against Godfather* before his untimely demise, Bruce mused on the effects of water on a city's creativity thus:

"Be like water making its way through cracks. Do not be assertive, but adjust to the object, and you shall find a way round or through it. If nothing within you stays rigid, outward things will disclose themselves.
Empty your mind, be formless. Shapeless, like water. If you put water into a cup, it becomes the cup. You put water into a bottle and it becomes the bottle. You put it in a teapot it becomes the teapot. Now, water can flow or it can crash. Be water, my friend."

Well, it couldn't be much clearer. Be water, my friends. Be Amsterdam.

The Pedalo
For some reason it's always strange to see one of these outside the Costa del Sol. Yet as the pedalo combines water and cycling (well, pedalling at least) it could be hailed as the most 'Amsterdam' form of transport on the water. It's certainly not the most dignified, though that never worried John much, a man never happier than putting the pedalo to the metal.

HOW TO GET INTO THE FLOW IN AMSTERDAM

The most popular way to ease yourself into Amsterdam's water system is on one of the city's infamous canal cruises. Yes, you'll be distinctly in tourist territory here, but there must be some reason why seemingly everyone connected with Amsterdam will advise you to go on one of these tours. Maybe, as with so many things, people don't want to think beyond the first thing that comes to mind (John, obviously, is the honourable exception to this rule) but in this instance people may have a point, because seeing Amsterdam from the water is different, even exciting. It's almost worth putting up with hearing the same sentence repeated in about fifteen different languages on the running commentary supplied by the cruise companies.

If, however, you do feel that a jaunt through the canals is an indispensable part of your Amsterdam experience, then John's tour operator of choice would undoubtedly be Lovers. Yes, Lovers. That's really what they're called. Lovers is the name, taking you through the canals of Amsterdam is their game. But there is one thing that Lovers offer that sets them apart from every other canal cruiser in town, and that's the coolest boat in the history of the world ever. Really. It's so special that it would make even Steve Zissou jealous.

It's an amphibious superduper bus slash boat that drives you from Schiphol Airport to the centre of Amsterdam before diving into the water and giving you a quick tour of the city. Yes, a quick (and therefore instantly more appealing than the other lengthy tours offered by inferior operators) tour of the city on the same bus that half an hour earlier had been driving on the motorway but that is now in the water. Amazing. How can you not love it? The icing on this particularly appealing cake is that this marvellous machine is called the Floating Dutchman (do you see what they did there?). This is the real deal. However, despite the manifold charms of the Floating Dutchman, John would still advise that you explore a more *gezellig* option of navigating Amsterdam's canal and secure passage on a private boat.

PLEASURE BOATS
Having a boat in Amsterdam is perhaps the ultimate status symbol. No matter whether it's a dinghy or a top of the range sloep, if you're able to float your own boat (and pay the

The Sup
What SUP? The Stand Up Paddle board apparently, the latest craze to make waves in the water sport world. It's even reached Amsterdam, despite the distinct lack of swell. Happily with the SUP board, surf is always up. Gnarly, as John would say.

exorbitant mooring fees) you'll be the envy of everyone in town. It won't have escaped your notice that we've assembled an Altman guide (a boatspotter's guide if you will) in this chapter to most of the boats you're likely to see around town, allowing you to pick your boat of choice before you arrive. Because if you can secure passage on one, the superior manner to enjoy Amsterdam's canals is undoubtedly from a private boat. That's to say a boat of which you know the captain and can share the boat with a bunch of friends while not paying over the odds for food and drink.

But if you're worried that boating might be a bit too much like hard work, fret not. Because boating in Amsterdam is completely different from sailing. Sailing involves a lot of effort, skill, concentration and even a spot of practice every now and then. Whereas boating involves sitting on a boat while someone keeps a gentle hand on the rudder to ensure that you don't stray into the path of another boat. That's about it. The only thing you risk straining while boating is your bladder and the most exerting thing you'll have to do is tax your mind as to where and when you'll get off the boat to go to the loo.

Basically all you'll do is sit on a boat in the sun with your friends, eat, drink and make merry while contemplating nature from a slowly meandering boat. Life doesn't get much better. When boating, it doesn't really matter where you go, and you certainly won't go anywhere very quickly, but one of the best things you can do on a boat in Amsterdam is get out of there. The traffic on the canals can reach titanic proportions at the height of summer, which isn't totally pleasant, and as there's so much else to see outside the city, it would be a shame to confine yourself to Amsterdam's city limits. Within half an hour (that's absolutely no time on a boat, believe me) you can be in the middle of the Dutch countryside.

Swing out of the canal district, hang a right down the river Ij and you'll find Ouderkerk aan de Amstel. It's a picturesque village that's pretty unremarkable in itself, but on the way there are cows, dykes, fields, windmills and tulips aplenty. You'll be spoilt for choice as to which Dutch cliché you choose to rest your eye upon. And if at any time you want to stop off for a swim or a bite to eat, well, there are opportunities and time aplenty for that too.

The only piece of practical advice that John would give is that you should always be careful when detaching the rudder at the end of the day, or while handling any of your personal effects

The Canal Cruise Boat

We've included this so you'll know exactly which kind of boat to avoid. There is however one that we'd like to draw to your attention - The Pannenkoek Boat. Pannenkoek is Dutch for pancake and the Pannenkoek Boat is therefore a boat that serves pancakes.

If you're Dutch (and even if you're not), this is probably as good as it gets - Amsterdam, boats and pancakes combined in one monument to everything's that good in the world. It's so good that you'd have to be a pannenkoek to miss it (yes, pannenkoek is Dutch slang for 'mad'. Those crazy Dutch!)

that won't float in water, otherwise you'll have to go fishing to retrieve them. After one particularly fluid trip we had on the canals, somehow the rudder of the ship, instead of being safely packed away, ended up slipping into the murky depths of the canal while everybody looked on helplessly. A boat without a rudder is, um, rudderless, meaning we had to spend half an hour doing our best to recover it. And it might just have worked if it hadn't been cold, dark (and distinctly wet) and our attempts hadn't consisted mainly of diving to the bottom, sticking our hands in the mud briefly to get cut by bottles and goodness knows what else, before resurfacing a couple of seconds later. All in all, we'd have better off doing what John would have done in the same situation: nothing. Then none of us would have got that nasty rash in that rather sensitive place that takes some explaining to your wife after a weekend in Amsterdam. Yep, sometimes doing less really is doing more.

It could be difficult to meet someone Dutch with a boat, but most people with a boat here are so proud of them that if you hang around long enough in a bar and drop enough hints about what you're after someone will be only too happy to offer you passage on their tub, especially if you flash some Euros (or some of the Dutch you've learned) around.

The Botel
If you want the full hit of the boat experience, then the Botel is the place to be. It's a boat (well, obviously, otherwise it wouldn't be in this chapter) and it's a hotel! You could even say it's a ferry nice hotel if you wished. It's moored just over the way from Centraal Station, so to get to the mainland and back you have to get another boat. Thus boats could be the only form of transport you need to take in the city. Wahey.

Bogurtuin, Java Island.
A good spot for an outdoor swim is Bogurtuin, opposite Centraal Station. N.B. John doesn't advocate diving into the water without due care and attention. Well, sometimes maybe.

Otherwise your best shot of getting on board a boat is to wait until April 30th, otherwise known as Queen's day. You'll probably have heard about this as the day when everyone in Amsterdam dons orange and the city turns into one giant street party to honour the Queen's official birthday. So to escape this, everyone who has a boat or access to one runs to their boat, fills it with as much booze and food as possible and takes to the canals to get away from it all. Which as everyone else does the same thing means that there's total gridlock on the canals and any form of movement is virtually impossible. Which isn't necessarily a bad thing, nor is it a particularly good thing, especially if you need to answer the call of nature, a call that becomes particularly fierce if you've been drinking all day, as everyone is apt to do on Queen's Day.

You can of course get off the boat and throw yourself upon the mercy of some kind Dutch person who has a nearby house and will charge you five measly Euros for the privilege. Or you can just go for a pee in the streets and hope that no one notices. Which still leaves you caught short if you're a lady. But luckily the Dutch have thought of everything, and if I say the words 'she-pee', hopefully everything will become crystal clear. If not, Google it. I think it's brilliant (but then I'm a man and I've never had to use it. It sounds brilliant though. Brilliant.) Anyway, getting back to Queen's Day. The other funny, well, mildly diverting thing about boats is that you're not allowed to drink and drive while in charge of a boat. Bicycles, yes, boats, no. Which poses a slight problem on Queen's Day when everyone is out of their skull on drink, drugs and love for Queen Beatrix. But don't imagine for one moment that the Dutch police take the day off, no sir. So sail with caution (not too close to the wind therefore), otherwise you might end up with a rather sizeable fine. Again.

DOING NOTHING ON THE WATER WITH NOTHING

But don't worry, it's not like you need a boat to do nothing by the water in Amsterdam, because one of the best things to do by the water is nothing. To sit down and contemplate nature or the surroundings and watch the world go by. And Amsterdam, as a city full of water, offers plenty of opportunities to do this. There's always a chance to stop and have a sandwich, write a poem, or have a think, just around the corner. The best way to find a spot is just to look for a canal (it shouldn't be hard) and wander up and down it until you find a place that whispers 'stop.' One place that it's particularly easy to stay an extended amount of time at on the water is the Noorderlicht café in Amsterdam Noord. You'll need to get the ferry to the NDSM

Werf – it'll cost you ten minutes but zero Euros – but boy is it worth it. It's got a garden that faces Amsterdam Centraal with a panoramic view of the river and the rest of the city (the mainland if you will) that you can drink in for hours. The bar itself is also very nice with friendly staff, decent food (and barbecues in the summer), occasional musical nights and it's all relatively easy on the wallet. It's a winner.

SWIMMING

There's one more thing that we'd like to say about Amsterdam's 165 (yes, count them, 165) canals that together constitute more than 100 kilometres of lovely water. Water, as every proud resident of Amsterdam and representative of the city council will be keen to tell you, that is clean enough to swim in. Which is exactly what we're going to advise you to do now. Really. The people who manage Amsterdam's water are going all out to make it even cleaner – maybe not clean enough to drink, but certainly good enough for a quick dip. There are even boats that go and up down the canals picking up the vast amount of detritus that gets dumped into them (including, of course, bicycles) and every day, between the hours of 19.30 and 20.30, 600,000 m^3 of lovely, clean, fresh water is pumped through Amsterdam's canal system to help purify it.

Whether the water is genuinely so clean as we're led to believe is another matter, but it won't kill you to try. There's something undeniably romantic and liberating about plunging into a canal right in the middle of a city. And you won't be alone in doing it, as on balmy sunny days the canals team with children diving happily into the Amstel, a sight to gladden even the most jaded and aquaphobic of hearts. And if you were after any reassurance about the potential health risks of swimming in the Amstel, just look how tall and robustly healthy everyone is here. There really must be something in the water…

EEN BROODJE WARM VLEES EN PINDASAUS

(That's a warm meat and peanut sauce roll, and that explains how doing (or eating) nothing is the key to eating well in Amsterdam)

WHERE WOULD JOHN GO TO EAT IN AMSTERDAM?

As you'd expect from a man who makes his own cookies, John is a man for whom food, and good food, is a pretty big deal. No more so than on holiday, which he sees as one big trip for his taste buds. Which brings us seamlessly to Amsterdam. And Dutch food.

It's somewhat of an unknown quantity in the rest of the world. I mean, we all know about Dutch cheese (Edam, Babybel) and er, that's about it. Ask someone Dutch about their food however, and they'll wax lyrical about the wonders of their national cuisine. Een broodje kaas, stamppot, kipsaté, kroket, erwtensoep, poffertjes, these are dishes that the very mention of will set Dutch mouths salivating. Whether you'll find them as delectable, we'll endeavour to discover together on our own voyage through Dutch cuisine.

DUTCH FOOD

There's an old gag about Dutch food, that there are two food groups in Dutch cooking: bread, and things that go on bread. Somewhat surprisingly, it's a joke that's wasted on Dutch audi-

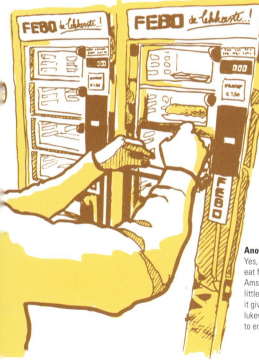

Another snack from the wall
Yes, as you'll learn, it's possible to eat food out of a vending machine in Amsterdam. If you put money in (a little over a Euro is usually enough), it gives you the right to take out a lukewarm snack of dubious quality to enjoy on the spot. Mmm, lekker!

ences. Partly because it's a gross generalisation but principally because the Dutch are a tiny bit touchy about the merits of their cuisine. It's not that they think that what they eat is the best in the world (well, maybe just a teeny bit), more that they're very happy with what they've got, thank you very much indeed, especially if it's a meal based around meat, potatoes and vegetables. Or cheese. Or bread, obviously.

The Dutch passion for food runs so deep that the appearance of anything edible is inevitably greeted with the word *'lekker'*. *Lekker* (as you'll know if you've paid suitable attention to your Dutch lessons) means 'delicious', a definition that you might find hard to credit when it's applied to something as run of the mill as a cheese sandwich or a piece of sausage. Yet *lekker* these humble items most certainly are and always will be, just like something truly spectacular as, I don't know, a nice Parmigiana or a spot of proper cordon bleu cooking.

The best way to interpret this attitude to food is as the ultimate example of the famous Dutch open-mindedness – the fact that almost everything can be *lekker* shows a radical lack of fussiness and pretension that the rest of the world could do well to emulate. However, if you're sticking to your guns on the whole 'I actually care about what I eat and don't want to eat any old crap' thing, we've picked out a few Dutch specialities to help you navigate your way through this culinary minefield.

BREAD

As we started with that throwaway gag (don't worry, we're nearing the end of the book now so there aren't too many more of those to come) about bread, we should probably explain it. The Dutch are indeed fond of bread, and it will form the basis of most lunches and breakfasts that you'll be offered. At both meals you're likely to be confronted with a fresh loaf of bread (or rolls) and an array of spreads, slices and condiments to adorn your sandwich with.

If that doesn't get your juices flowing, well, I'm afraid you're in for a tough time here. But perhaps I can excite you by saying that bread is something that the Dutch take very seriously and therefore something that they do pretty well. It's always freshly made and consumed and it normally tastes of something, thus raising it immediately far above the English variety in the taste charts, if not quite doing enough to trouble the French and Italians at the top of the tree.

But while many Dutch people will be more than happy to wax eloquent on the subject of bread, for John it was what you put on your bread that matters. Which leads us neatly to cheese, the element that almost no Dutch meal is complete without: breakfast (in the form of a ham and cheese croissant or a currant bun with a slice of cheese in the middle), lunch (a cheese sandwich, what else?) and dinner (a witlof and cheese salad perhaps, a dish that's especially beloved here as witlof, a sort of root chicory, is a big Dutch favourite).

Of course, for many unenlightened people Dutch cheese will forever be synonymous with Edam, but there is much more to Dutch cheese than that - or so they'd have you believe. In fact, Dutch cheese is right up there with Dutch cycling skills and ice skating on the Dutch list of 'Things we do very well if in fact we're not the best in the world at this kind of thing'.

When presented with an example of this expertise in the form of a piece of yellow cheese that seems to assume the texture of rubber when placed in your mouth, foreigners might find this pride rather hard to appreciate (or stomach), but I'd say you just need to file this under 'acquired tastes', especially if you want to make any friends here, as criticising Dutch cheese just doesn't go down well in the Netherlands. A general rule of thumb would be to avoid any 'Jong' or young cheese and stick to old cheese, 'Oude Kaas', the stuff that actually tastes of something and isn't (as) rubbery. And no matter how tempted you are, don't be tempted by the cheese with bacon or cheese with herbs. That's why books like this exist, so we taste this stuff on your behalf and you can forego the pain of having a) to eat it and b) be polite about it in front of your new Dutch friends.

In fact the best thing you could do is pay a visit to one of the two finest cheese shops in Amsterdam, lovingly run

The Kaasschaaf
The Dutch use this to cut cheese. They're incredibly proud of it. If you listen to them, they'll tell you that they use it as a thin slice of cheese tastes much better than a thick slice. But deep down they know they do it because they're too tight to give someone a nice, big fat lump of cheese...

by people who give Dutch cheese the care and attention it deserves. The Kaaskamer, in the heart of the 9 Straatjes is one; Kaashandel Kef in West Amsterdam is the other. Here you can experience (and eat) Dutch cheese at its finest and discover what all the fuss is about.

STREET FOOD

Apparently street food is the 'in thing' right now. The flavour of the month, you could say. No travel guide is complete without a section on it, we were reliably informed. Well, let no one say that John Altman is a man to lag behind the times. Food is indeed available to purchase and consume on the streets of Amsterdam and therefore more than eligible for inclusion in our modest tome. And because we like to balance the sweet with the sour, the rough with the smooth (it's a karma thing), we'll share with you both the acceptable and the not quite so acceptable, but really not that bad, faces of Amsterdam street food. Beginning with the herring.

Herring is big business in Amsterdam. As with so much in the Netherlands, it has its roots in the Golden Age. After all, if you're on a boat for a long time, like between the Netherlands and Japan for example, then the only way to ensure a plentiful supply of food is to preserve it in salt. Thus was the herring, a fish preserved in salt, born. By the way, you might not know that the Netherlands was the only non-Asian country allowed to trade with Japan between 1633 and 1853. I didn't either until I read David Mitchell's wonderful book *The Thousand Autumns of Jacob de Zoet*. I suggest you do, too.

WHERE WOULD JOHN GO?

How to eat herring
This is a herring. Many people would have you believe that this fish is as good as it gets as regards eating in Amsterdam. We'll tell you more about it later, so let this little text serve as a little soupçon to whet your appetite ahead of the main dish. Herring is always consumed raw and therefore best enjoyed fresh (fresh from the knife as the Dutch say) at one of Amsterdam's many herring stalls.

Anyway, to return to the herring. This is how it goes: the fish is caught, normally before the breeding season in May. It's then preserved in salt in a barrel to keep it fresh. The freshest fish are the first catch of the season, the fabled *Hollandse Nieuwe*, that are available in May-July from the *haringkraam*, the stalls where herring can be purchased for your delectation. Wisdom holds that herring starts losing its flavour the second it's opened up, so you should insist (well, ask politely) that your herring is cleaned and sliced in front of you. That way you know it's properly fresh. Good herring should look slightly red and bloody and be firm in texture. Bad herring is grey, looks a bit grim and tastes even worse.

Stubbe's Haring
There are a lot of good places to find herring in Amsterdam, but there's quite a few bad ones as well. So to be sure you experience the herring at its finest, head to Stubbe's Haring. You'll find it straddling the Haarlingersluis at the start of the Singel, next to the Harlemmermeer, five minutes away from Centraal Station. The Stubbe family have been running it since 1903 and their herring is 'legendary' according to JA himself. John hated being called JA by the way, but for reasons of space we call him JA every now and then. Sorry, John.

Welcome to the Snackbar

A good friend of John's, a certain Rogier van de Swag, was vegetarian and unbending in his resolution to let no meat pass his lips. Except that is, whenever he was tempted by a kroket. Then, it pains me to say, Rogier could hold back no longer and would devour the kroket in sheer ecstasy, casting aside his principles and ignoring its meat content to sate his lust for the most lekker of all Dutch snacks. That, ladies and gentlemen, is the power snackbar cuisine exerts over its clientele, both willing and unwilling. Across the next few pages we'll lay out the delights available in these temples of fried cuisine so that you too can become familiar with the frikandel, the kroket, the broodje bal, the rookworst and more.

Once you've got hold of a good herring, all you need to worry about is whether you want onions with it and if you choose to eat it whole or in bits. The traditional school of thought is that onions merely distract from the full hit of the herring flavour and should therefore be avoided, and that you should consume it whole by lowering it into your mouth - it looks good for the cameras if nothing else. But, as ever with John, however you feel comfortable doing it is the way to go.

The last Dutch dish you should definitely try is stamppot. It's a sort of mashed potato dish that incorporates green vegetables, carrot (sometimes), sausage, cheese and mashed potato, natch. If you're feeling particularly adventurous you can even chuck some fruit into the mix (banana and pineapple work particularly well), or some *zuurkool* (sauerkraut, or given the Dutch aversion to comparing Dutch things with German things, let's call it pickled cabbage). Stamppot is a Dutch classic right up there with cheese on the scale of national affection. It's simple, warming and filling, Dutch food at it's best. That's not a diss, it's a compliment from the bottom of my heart. If you wished

Kroket The king of Dutch snackbar cuisine. For readers already familiar with brown cafés a kroket's a bit like bitterballen, but bigger and more satisfying. Just like bitterballen, it's served ridiculously hot and best consumed in a roll with mustard and ketchup.

Thus the kroket might seem like a simple dish but it's not. It comes in almost as many varieties as the sauces that accompany the chips: veal, goulash, vegetarian, meat, even saté flavour (that's peanut sauce, in case you'd forgotten) is available.

to ham it up a little you could even say it's the Dutch character expressed in a meal – uncomplicated, welcoming, slightly strange at first but inexplicably addictive once you get used to it. And in autumn and winter you can now even get stamppot to take away thanks to a couple of fine institutions called Stamppotje – which in the summer double as decent ice cream shops (Ijscuypje), thus satisfying the Dutch cravings for highly starchy products throughout the year.

THE LESS ACCEPTABLE FACE OF AMSTERDAM STREET FOOD

A long time ago I was taken on a work trip to what we were reliably informed was the best place to eat local food, freshly prepared using local ingredients. The ideal place to eat in other words. To add to the romance of the situation, we were told it was to be found in a tent by the river, leading me to have a romantic vision of a fisherman's hut serving freshly caught fish served straight from the net. Instead once we turned off the Amsterdam ring road we were confronted with what the Dutch somewhat charmingly call a large 'partytent', but what in English we know as a gazebo, in which there was to be found a large man standing by an even larger deep fat fryer and in front of a vast freezer cabinet.

This was to be my first trip into a snackbar (sadly it wasn't my

Patat Chips/French Fries/Freedom Fries, whatever you want to call them it's essential that in Amsterdam you douse these slices of fried potato in sauce. Lots of sauce. Amongst the glorious variety of condiments available to you, we'd like to draw your attention to one in particular: patatje oorlog. Oorlog means war - a slightly controversial choice of word, admittedly, but one that makes sense when you learn that it describes peanut butter sauce mixed with mayonnaise with little bits of onions sprinkled on the top as well. It's a term that could only be improved upon by the politically correct, who wanted 'war' changed to 'party.' Needless to say it didn't catch on. Patatje oorlog on the other hand, did. There's no accounting for taste…

last) and I was unfamiliar with the food on offer and how one should go around ordering. So I asked the forbidding 'chef' towering a good metre above me what he recommended. "It's all good" he grunted, before rearranging his wares in front of me. Cheers, mate. So that you won't have run the same gauntlet, we've compiled a guide to the treats that you can expect to find within one of Amsterdam's many neon-lit emporiums of fried delights. You'll see it throughout this chapter wherever you spot an illustration of a piece of food that looks good enough to eat accompanied by a particularly witty bit of text.

THE LEKKERSTE SNACKBARS

In Amsterdam there are two particular names we'd like to draw to your attention in the snackbar world – Febo and The World's First Organic Snackbar. The latter speaks for itself,

Een broodje warm vlees met pindasaus
This a roll filled with warm slices of meat (the type of animal it comes from generally isn't specified) slathered in peanut sauce. It's a speciality of the Broodje Mokum, a rather endearing café on the Rozengracht that's staunchly, and proudly, 'Amsterdam' (Mokum is slang for Amsterdam) and restricts itself to serving about six things, one of which is this delicacy. If you like meat and peanuts, you'll be in heaven. If not, stay away.

EEN BROODJE WARM VLEES EN PINDASAUS

Frikandel The frikandel recently celebrated its 50th anniversary. Beyond this, little is known about this perennial snackbar favourite, and nor should you endeavour to learn more, since the less you know the better if you really want to enjoy this slice of, um, stuff. Broadly speaking it's a kind of sausage. A bit longer and a bit thinner, but frankly god knows what else goes into it.
It's also available as Frikandel Speciaal, which involves slicing the frikandel open, liberally applying mayonnaise and ketchup all over it before sprinkling some onions on top, and voila, you've got yourself something truly special.

a wonderful paradox found in West Amsterdam that uses organic ingredients for everything then fries the bejesus out of them.

While the Febo is a genuine Amsterdam phenomenon – it gets its name from its original location on the Ferdinand Bolstraat in the Pijp. Their slogan, as befitting the finest and most beloved of snackbar cuisine is, 'de lekkerste' (the most *lekker*) and they take great pride in preparing their food fresh every day before, again, frying the bejesus out of it. But most of their appeal for us foreigners lies in their status as the largest, most immediate purveyor of food from the wall. Yes, as you'll have noticed from the fetching portrait of John at the start of this chapter, in Amsterdam it's possible to eat warm food from a vending machine set in a wall. If you've been to Japan, this might not seem that strange. I've never been to Japan but it still seems strange. It's quite simple really, you put money into the wall, a couple of second later you open the flap and take your choice of tepid food out. The first time it's exciting, the second time, well, the novelty wears off as quickly as the flavour. My favourite thing about the Febo though is the sign on the branch by the Leidseplein welcoming every visitor to the

Broodje Bal A big ball of meat, normally served (whole) in a bun with gravy. It's a dubious pleasure and about as hard to digest as it is to fit in your mouth. John would advise slicing said ball into pieces rather than trying to force it into your mouth in one go.

home of Dutch cuisine, thus explicitly confirming that you are indeed enjoying the finest food that Amsterdam has to offer.

EATING OUT

You know, like in a restaurant and everything. Because sometimes it's nice to give yourself a bit of a treat. Generally Amsterdam is a strange city to eat in. Café culture is strong, but restaurant culture less so. The Dutch like eating at home (it's more *gezellig*) and given that eating out is relatively expensive (you'll struggle to find many dishes coming in at less than fifteen Euros) and as Dutch people hate loosening their purse strings, it makes sense for them to eat at home. However, the positive side of this is that unless you go to a really fancy restaurant, you shouldn't pay more than twenty Euros for a very good main course.

The challenge therefore lies in sorting the wheat from the chaff. As with every capital city, especially one as thrustingly creative as Amsterdam, there are a lot of restaurants that try far too hard to impress. They experiment with food too much and

EEN BROODJE WARM VLEES EN PINDASAUS

Hema Worst Hema is an institution that rivals only the snackbar in the affections of the Dutch people. It's a high street store that stocks everything from underpants to smoothies and its mission is to sell good quality products at a reasonable price. But what we're here for is their sausage, the legendary Hema Worst. It's a large piece of sausage served in a roll with a dash of mustard. You might know it as a hot dog, but to the Dutch it's the finest sausage treat in the whole world. And at two euros, who's going to argue?

somehow as the experimentation level goes up, so the size of the portion and the level of enjoyment goes down.

The Amsterdam twist on this is the city's apparent appetite for fusion cooking. Although John was fond of experimenting with cookies (the beer and caramel cookies he once baked still give all of us who were lucky enough to taste it a sunshine feeling on a rainy day) anything he made was the result of a careful and rigorous research into the karmic properties of every ingredient. In Amsterdam however, restaurateurs throw karma out of the kitchen door to present you with some of the most bizarre combinations of international cuisines imaginable – Chinese and Indian food, Dutch and, well, food from anywhere. None of them beat the Pizza/Sushi/Chinese restaurant I once ate at in Milan but still, these places should be avoided at all costs.

The kind of restaurants John would favour are the ones that concentrate on doing on thing really well. Places like Café Amsterdam, on the Watertorenplein near the Westerpark, which serves good, simple food in beautiful surroundings, and Rosa and Rita in East, which serves only pizza or steak. Or any of the restaurants that focus on offering one of the many national cuisines that Amsterdam offers. As the city's tourist board is fond of telling you, the widest variety of nationalities in the world live here, and a good portion of them are represented in the city's dining options.

The very best of these options are largely based on the food of the Netherlands' former colonies. Indonesian food, together with Surinamese food, provides the only real injection of spice and flavour you're likely to find in the city and both are really worth investigating, Indonesian food especially. At an Indonesian restaurant you'd be best off ordering a rijsttafel, sitting down and doing little else but working your way through its

The best way to find Café Amsterdam is by looking for the water tower that, um, towers, over the surrounding area. It's still in use, in case you're interested, serving as a water reserve and a buffer in case of a drop in pressure, just as it always has.

Café Amsterdam
Sadly in real life it's not marked by a nice big arrow as in this diagram, but hopefully the water tower will help you find your way here.

EEN BROODJE WARM VLEES EN PINDASAUS

Some like it hot. Most people here don't
In most places if people ask if the food is spicy, it's because they want it even spicier. In Amsterdam it's because if the answer to the question is 'yes,' it means that it's a signal to steer well clear of the dish in question. Because despite the multitude of cuisines from around the globe available in Amsterdam, the one thing you won't be able to find is some proper spicy food. You can try and ask for it 'extra spicy,' but years of catering for the Dutch market have ensured that even the most adventurous of restaurateurs have downgraded the status 'extra spicy' for the Dutch palate to a heat that is merely 'mild' for the rest of the world. So if you want some kick to your food, either bring your own Tabasco (or a Madame Jeanette pepper as pictured left) with you, or wait till you get home.

many delights for a good couple of hours. A rijsttafel is 'a rice table' and consists of a selection of about ten or more small dishes. Apparently it came into existence when the Dutch went to Indonesia for the first time and asked (okay, commanded) the locals to cook something for them. The Dutch weren't impressed with the initial offerings (it was probably too spicy), so asked the villagers to lay on everything they could provide.

Gashouder, Westergasfabriek
We've talked a lot about the Westerpark in this book. Well, now you can finally see a part of it in the form of its iconic gas holder. Amazingly, the Westerpark is as close to the water tower opposite as it is in this book (scale 1:100), meaning that after spending all day chilling in the park you just have to stroll across the bridge to round off the perfect day in West with a meal at Café Amsterdam.

And thus was the rice table brought into existence. True story. Perhaps.

Anyway, you'll find a particularly good Indonesian restaurant in the form of Blauw near the Vondelpark. Or if you're after a more down to earth Indonesian, try Bojos on the Lange Leidsedwarsstraat. The food is good, if not spectacular, the décor has to be seen to be believed and the people running it are delightful. And if you're after some Surinamese food, it's generally held that you can find the best roti in town at Lalla Rookh, near Muiderpoort Station in East Amsterdam. The rest of your culinary voyage through Amsterdam we'll leave in your own good hands. *Eet smakelijk!*

EEN BROODJE WARM VLEES EN PINDASAUS

Where John Wouldn't Go

(That tells you how to get out of some tight spots and shows you some much nicer places to do nothing rather than something)

As you've probably gathered by now, John's the kind of guy who would try anything once, a man who was happy to go wherever the wind blew him. But it pains us to relate there are some parts of Amsterdam that even someone with the most open of minds and placid of temperaments wouldn't touch with a bargepole.

So to help ensure that you continue to have nothing but fond memories of your time in Amsterdam we've compiled a list of all the places you're better off avoiding together with a series of corresponding get out of jail free cards – so whether you get bored of waiting in a queue or just want to see the other side of Amsterdam, you'll be just a handy suggestion away from somewhere infinitely preferable. And at the very least you'll know when (and how firmly) to say no if someone has the temerity to suggest going somewhere as mind-numbingly tedious as the Heineken Experience.

THE RED LIGHT DISTRICT
We'll get the most obvious one out of the way immediately. For if there's one place that it's hard to understand the appeal of in Amsterdam, it's the Red Light District. This isn't because of any attempt to seize the moral high ground (despite the general exploitation of women) it's just hard, if not impossible, to understand why so many tourists are drawn here. Admittedly the general cultural novelty value of exploring an area where prostitution is legal is pretty high, but in reality the Red Light District is a seedy, unpleasant place to be.

It's starved of sunshine even at the height of summer, meaning that the atmosphere never really rises above gloomy, especially when night falls and the galaxy of neon lights are switched on, an effect that instead of illuminating the area only makes it dingier. Given the general unattractiveness of the area, it's no surprise that Amsterdam's city council has been trying relatively vigorously to clean it up in the last few years by reducing the number of windows (that's the not-so technical term for a place where a prostitute works) and encouraging visitors from abroad to come here for other reasons than drug and sex tourism. It's a stance that even someone as defiantly liberal as John approves of wholeheartedly.

However all that tourist trade has to go somewhere, so to ensure that it would still flow to the Dutch purse there was talk of establishing a 'Sin City' somewhere in the country, a city that would be full of brothels, coffeeshops (with catering by McDonalds you'd assume) and a highway to hell. Realistically this could only happen near Amsterdam, Eindhoven or Maastricht as that's where the major airports are in the Netherlands, but it's been five years since these rumours first rumoured, meaning that they can now (regrettably) be filed away in the urban legend box. And in the meantime nothing much has happened, except that the boundaries of the Red Light District have been scaled down rather drastically.

There is one place within this wasteland that's worth a quick mention, the San Francisco - and no, we're not saying that just because that's where we met John. We're saying that because it's the only bar/club in the area that's open after 2 am. You'll find it half the way up the Zeedijk and it generally opens whenever everywhere else closes, which is handy as you wouldn't really want to go there in full possession of your capacities. The music is crap, the drinks are of dubious quality (but cheap), there's a dancefloor with fluorescent lights that moves in time with the music (or at least it seems that way at three o'clock in the morning) and the clientele are rowdy. So all in all, it's John's kind of place. As is Casablanca down the road, which is where you can get your karaoke on every Wednesday.

But ultimately we're going to stick to our guns and advise you just to get the hell out of the Red Light District. Literally, keep on going down the Oude Hoogstraat. Once you emerge

onto the Jodenbreestraat turn right, and after a couple of minutes you'll see a narrow, but tallish pub on a wharf. It's called the Sluyswacht and it's extremely *gezellig*, with a nice view over the canal and everything. Once you've washed off the taint of the Red Light District, we'd suggest you mosey on down the road towards the Waterlooplein and marvel at the Portuguese Synagogue, one of the most majestic buildings in the Dam.

ANNE FRANK HUIS

Next on the list of Amsterdam clichés to cross off your list is the Anne Frank Huis. Saying this feels a bit wrong, a bit like farting in church, but we're afraid we're going to do it anyway - tell you not to go the Anne Frank Huis, not fart in church, you'll be relieved to hear.

The main reason is the queues. The never-ending queues that begin as soon as the sun rises and are still going strong as it sets. Besides this, the whole thing feels a bit ghoulish, almost as voyeuristic in its own way as the Red Light District. Of course, we haven't got a bad word to say about Anne Frank or the work of the Anne Frank Foundation. She's an inspirational figure whose life serves as a lesson

to us all. However I can't help but feel that her memory is best served by reading the book and investigating the history rather than buying a ticket to see the place where she and her family were incarcerated. There's just something a bit ghoulish about the whole thing.

Instead, you could cross the road to the Westerkerk and have a quick look at the Homo Monument, a tribute to all the gay men and women killed in the second world war and all those who have been (and continue to be) persecuted since time immemorial.

Or for something completely different - if you're after a more permanent souvenir of your time in Amsterdam - head to Marnixstraat to get a tattoo by Emiel Steenhuizen, John's favourite tattoo artist. You'll find him at Admiraal Tattoo. Emiel's the one with a beard and a winning smile. Great minds think alike, John always said, although unlike John Emiel normally wears more than an apron when he's at work. A good job really.

MADAME TUSSAUDS

Why people go here I really have absolutely no idea. I thought London was the only city in the world to be afflicted by Mrs Tussaud's wax creations (is this where the origin of the word 'wack' comes from? We should be told.), but no, Amsterdam caught the bug too - together with most of the major cities of the world it transpired after further investigation. Why, God only knows. It's a mystery up there with the popularity of Peruvian flute bands - watch *South Park* if you want to get to the bottom of that particular mystery. Even the people in the queue look like that they don't know why they're there. To be fair you'll probably see a version of Justin Bieber with more charisma than the real Beeb. I mean, if you think you should go there, then please write in and tell us why. We're all ears.

Fortunately for the rest of us, you've got the joys of the 9 Straatjes ready and waiting for you, a small district of nine streets spread between the Keizersgracht, Prinsengracht and Herengracht overflowing with shops, cafés, bars, places to eat and other lovely stuff to help you spend your money and your time in a much more constructive and rewarding manner than gawping at Mark Rutte (the Dutch Prime Minister).

THE HEINEKEN EXPERIENCE
It's not really exaggerating to say that this is as close as Amsterdam comes to hell on earth. Okay, perhaps that is going a little bit over the top, and it's a title that the Rembrandtplein deserves, but at least you don't have to pay to go there. At The Heineken Experience, you have to shell out sixteen Euros to endure an hour of unrelenting Heineken advertising with only two piddly glasses of beer to reward you at the end. It's enough to turn you teetotal. The only useful bit of the trip is when they teach you how to drink beer properly, but by this point in your life you should have mastered this basic skill of drinking out of a glass a long, long time ago.

Yet for someone unknown reason a disproportionately high level of Amsterdam tourists are drawn here. They can be spotted proudly sporting their green bracelets and toting large green bags of Heineken swag. Perhaps they're drawn here because they heard that back in the day rather than two glasses of beer, you were granted twenty minutes free drinking time in the bar – a period that was extending to forty minutes if you took the first tour of the day at 9 o'clock in the morning. Which of course we did, and the amount of beer we managed to quaff just about made up for what we'd endured beforehand. Anyway, now that that perk has gone the way of the dodo, you'd be better off scorning this temple to mammon and going somewhere the beer actually tastes of something and you're not assaulted by a marketing message every ten seconds.

Just around the corner from the Heineken Experience is the Gollem pub, or beer heaven as it's otherwise known. Simply turn left, take a four-minute stroll down the Ferdinand Bolstraat (ignoring the dubious charms of the Irish pub on the corner) and turn down Daniel Stalpertstraat. You'll need to keep your eyes peeled as it's a small, unprepossessing place that you might otherwise miss. But walk inside and you'll be welcomed by a truly inspiring array of Belgian beers (over 200 I believe) that unlike Heineken actually taste of some-

Kwak, Kwak
This is John's tipple of choice at the Gollem.
Despite the sturdy and reassuring look and feel of the wooden holder, it's surprisingly hard to drink out of it. We advise practice. Lots of practice.

WHERE WOULD JOHN GO?

Tuschinkski Cinema
Look at it, just look at it. What a magnificent building.

thing. John would plump for a glass of Kwak, mainly because it comes served in a wooden sort of test tube rack. It's the kind of beer that should be drunk wearing a monocle. Win win. But watch out, the beers served here are rather strong. So after a heavy session you might have trouble getting up from your stool. Luckily they do serve snacks such as bitterballen and other such treats to line your stomach, so God willing, you'll be okay.

Postscript: there is good Dutch beer available in Amsterdam – and good Dutch beer from Amsterdam too. It's called De Prael and the only negative thing I've got to say about it is that it's quite hard to track down. To enjoy it on draught, head to the farm in the Westerpark, or it's available bottled at Marqt organic supermarket or De Bierkoning, a beer store just behind Dam Square on the Paleisstraat. But it is well worth seeking it De Prael out, their *Johnny* is so good it could even be English.

THE HERMITAGE

This is one place I've not got a bad word to say about. It's a beautiful building on the banks of the Amstel, down the road from the Carré theatre, just across from the picturesque Magere Brug. It's a lovely stretch of the river. The Hermitage is the sister of the museum of the same name in St. Petersburg that has one of the largest collections of art in the known universe, so it's fair to say that there's almost always something worth seeing here. But rather than get involved in all that, I'd suggest you take advantage of the location, crack open a beer, sit on the dock of the bay and watch the world go by.

The most compelling reason to walk on by the Hermitage is to check out the Hortus Botanicus, one of the oldest botanical gardens in the world. It's truly beautiful. It opened back when the Dutch ruled the waves in the 17th and 18th century and brought back everything they found to the headquarters of the dastardly Dutch East India Company, which in turn founded this place. Besides the stunning tropical plants, there's also a butterfly house, in which you can stand and let the butterflies fly all round you. If you can get one to land on your finger, we'll give you a whole five Euros - subject to availability.

THE RIJKSMUSEUM

The renovation of this incredible building has been going on for about ten years. It's a crying shame because it's a truly beautiful building, a gothic/neo renaissance masterpiece designed by the same architect who gave us Amsterdam Centraal, which funnily enough is the other building in town which seems to spend the whole time under canvas. John registered his displeasure at the fact that it's been impossible to enjoy all of

Ajax's Twelfth Man
An Ajax supporting friend of John's would like to point out that Ajax have won the European Cup, Europe's most prestigious trophy, four times, a truly remarkable achievement. Despite Ajax's creation of The Ajax Experience, a tourist trap on the Rembrandtplein, the best way to experience the magic of Ajax is to go the ArenA and watch a game for real, not pay 18 Euros to watch a bunch of videos.

the Rijksmuseum's charms for so long by refusing to darken its doors until the renovation is properly and totally finished. Which will probably be never, so we'd like to invite you to join his peaceful protest and wile away the hours that you could be inside the museum on the sun drenched piece of lawn behind it, admiring the understated charms of the Concertgebouw.

Or if you want to boycott the area completely, John would suggest you investigate another Amsterdam icon – Ajax Football Club. Ajax is Amsterdam's football team. They used to be the best team in the world 30 years ago, they were the best team in Europe as recently as 17 years ago and they're still one of the best teams in the Netherlands, whenever there's a break in the incessant political infighting that goes on behind the scenes and they can concentrate on playing football. They're without a doubt the most popular team in the country, mainly because they've traditionally been the most successful, and the legacy of players like Johan Cruyff, Marco Van Basten and Martijn Reuser ensures that there will always be a romantic side to their history that PSV Eindhoven (their main financial rivals) will never have. And Ajax's kit is a lot cooler.

Getting hold of tickets for a game is a little bit tricky, as in theory you have to have a club card to be able to buy them and as that takes a month to be processed, you'll be best off looking at less, um, official channels. So your best bet is either to go for a low-interest game when the tickets go on general sale or watch a game on TV in a bar, where every game is shown. If you can somehow get a hold of a ticket, you should definitely go, as Ajax are one of those teams who either crush other teams or self-destruct, both scenarios that are guaranteed to whip up their supporters into mass hysteria. They've been used to winning all their lives, and if they don't, they really can't take it. So wear something red and white and if something good happens start shouting 'Joden' (pronounced Yoda, like the Jedi Master, except 'Joden' means Jews, a throwback to the days when Ajax's stadium was in the Jewish neighbourhood).

THE BLOEMENMARKT

The Bloemenmarkt is Amsterdam's famous flower market. Once upon a time it was the place where all of the tulips from Amsterdam were bought and sold. Now it's just a few people selling fairly standard tulip bulbs that you can find elsewhere in the city with much less hassle and for much less money. But if by some misfortune you do end up in the Bloemenmarkt, don't worry, you're within reach of two of Amsterdam's best galleries and its most impressive cinema.

Down the road on the Keizersgracht is Foam (which you may remember we talked about in *Doing Nothing Inside*) and Mediamatic, a sort of art gallery that always has some sort of interesting art/media installation going on. One of the most noteworthy was an exhibition about mortality in which you could have a picture taken of yourself in a coffin. Dead cool. Or if that's all a little morbid, you should head down to the Tuschinski cinema just off Rembrandtplein. It's a beautiful gothic art deco building in the style of the Amsterdam School, a group of architects responsible for some of the most eye-catching buildings in the Netherlands. The Tuschinski is a converted cinema, and the main screen, that used to be the theatre's auditorium, has to be one of the best places to see a film I've been privileged to sit in. It's stunning, the kind of place that should have black tie as a dress code. Although this could possibly be relaxed if you go to see something like *Toy Story 3*.

ALBERT CUYPMARKT

I don't know what it is with places that everyone tells you to go to, but they all suck. The Albert Cuypmarkt, THE market in Amsterdam perhaps encapsulates this more than anywhere else. It's meant to be a place to catch the hustle and bustle of the city as the denizens of Amsterdam buy their fruit and vegetables and catch up on the local gossip, where the stall holders always have a joke and a smile for everyone. You know, how it was in the good old days, as it has been for the last fifty years and how it still continues to be. Or at least that's what the Amsterdam Tourism board would like you to believe.

't Sluysje
That's how its regulars affectionately refer to the Sluyswacht pub. Contrary to its depiction here, it's not actually part of the Red Light District.

The reality is slightly more sobering, as much like the vast majority of street markets in Europe it's been taken over by stands selling smoothies, mobile phone accessories and Amsterdam beanies - okay, these you might find only in Amsterdam. And most annoyingly it's full of people who walk really, incredibly, maddeningly slowly leading to a wholly frustrating experience.

So, as already alluded to, if you want to go to a proper market, get yourself to the Ten Katemarkt in West or the Farmers' Market in the Noordermarkt (in the Jordaan). If you're unlucky enough to find yourself stuck in the human traffic jam in the Albert Cuypmarkt and looking for an escape route, I'd suggest you dive into the Badcuyp Music Centre at one end of the market. They do 'world' music, which basically means they put on interesting music nights and during the day they serve a decent lunch cheaply and the people are friendly. I'd get in here if I were you for a genuine Amsterdam experience. Or if the weather's nice, head south to the Sarphatipark, the most idiosyncratic park in Amsterdam.

AMSTERDAM CITY CENTRE

As we've told you many, many times, Amsterdam's a small city. You're probably sighing deeply at reading that observation again, but it bears repeating, especially in a section about seeing alternative parts of the city. Because most of the people that come to Amsterdam will only see the centre of it, which is a bit unfortunate given that it's so easy to see the rest of it. To be fair, it's an oversight that most people who live here are guilty of as well. I was once cycling to West Amsterdam, not even that far, to the Baarsjes, the bit just west of the city centre, behind two women speaking loudly in English - that's also one of the strange things about Amsterdam, you'll hear almost as much English being spoken here as Dutch itself. Anyway, one said to the other how much there was to do round here and that if she'd have known how nice it was in the Baarsjes, she'd have come here a long time before.

That's the thing with Amsterdam, and every other city in the world. You get out of it what you put in. The Dutch have a nice expression for this, which runs along the lines of 'you need to look further than your nose is long' - it sounds better in Dutch, believe me. It basically means that you should search beyond the obvious. So if there's one thing we'd like you to take away with you (to Amsterdam), it's that. To go further than the centre of town. To do nothing. And to enjoy yourself.

So, as the Pet Shop Boys said, go west. Or east, or south, or north. Just don't bother to do too much when you get there.

Where Would John Go?

The short answer is everywhere, except all those places that we mentioned in the *Where John Wouldn't Go* part. But although we said that we wanted to let you discover your favourite parts of Amsterdam for yourself, we thought it'd only be polite to give you some more details of some of the places we mentioned in passing. To, you know, spread the love a bit.

So without further ado, here's where John would go to…

BUY A COPY OF THIS BOOK (or any other book, like *What Would John Do?*, for example) The Athenaeum, Spui 14-16 www.athenaeum.nl

ENJOY A KOFFIE VERKEERD Podium Mozaiek, Bos en Lommerweg 191. www.podiummozaiek.nl

SIGN UP TO HAVE A CHANCE OF LIVING ANTI-KRAAK www.interveste.nl

SPEND A DAY IN A BROWN CAFÉ Café Krom, Utrechtsestraat 76. It hasn't changed since the 1930s and it's got a jukebox. Brilliant.

BUY JOHN ALTMAN COOKIES Marqt, Overtoom 21-25. www.marqt.com

DRINK (GOOD) BEER IN A WINDMILL Brouwerij 't IJ, Funenkade 7, www.brouwerijhetij.nl (open from 3pm to 8 pm).

SIT ON THE DOCK OF A BAY Café Roest, Czaar Peterstraat 213 (behind the big newspaper buildings) www.amsterdamroest.nl

BUY A PROPER BIG BARBECUE WITH THREE COOKING SECTIONS AND EVERYTHING www.molenkitchen.com

BUY MEAT AT SIEM VAN DER GRAGT'S ORGANIC BUTCHERS Elandsgracht 116a, www.siemvandergragt.nl

BUY VEGETABLES AT THE FARMER'S MARKET IN THE NOORDERMARKT. It's all good, but our favourite is the Kwikstaart. We just like the name. Every Saturday from 9am till 4pm. www.boerenmarktamsterdam.nl

WATCH A FILM AT THE MOVIES (OF COURSE). The Movies, Haarlemmerdijk 161-163. If you want to eat there, they offer a special meal/ticket combo and the bar's not bad either. www.themovies.nl

CATCH A MUSIC FESTIVAL There are three really good ones: 5 Days Off, offering every kind of music in every music venue in town in March; Pitch Festival, an electronic/hip hop/dubstep/everything festival in July: www.pitchfestival.nl
Amsterdam Roots, a world music festival spread across the city in June/July: www.amsterdamroots.nl

DO SOME RECORD SHOPPING Distortion Records, Westerstraat 277 (Recommended by $jammie the Money, record digger and Amsterdam DJ de choix). www.distortion.nl

BUY SOME SPECIAL CLOTHES BY A CUTTING EDGE DUTCH DESIGNER Restored, Haarlemmerdijk 39 (Recommended by Femke Agema, a cutting edge Dutch designer). www.restored.nl

BUY SOME GLOVES OR AN UMBRELLA IN A HURRY Hema. You'll find these all over town - just dive into one to buy emergency protection against the weather. www.hema.nl

ENJOY THE BEST VIEW OF AMSTERDAM WITH A DRINK Canvas, Wibautstraat 150. www.canvas7.nl

TREAT HIMSELF AND SOMEONE SPECIAL TO A REALLY FANCY MEAL De Kas, Kamerlingh Onneslaan 3, www.restaurantdekas.nl (you might need to reserve this one).

GET HIS BIKE FIXED if you get a puncture, you'll want to go to the closest fietsenmaker (bike shop) possible. Luckily there's one on almost every corner. But one place we'll heartily recommend is the Fiets Consult, Utrechtsedwarsstraat. They're friendly, quick and cheap, and it's near Café Krom so you can have a drink while you wait. www.fietsconsult.nl

EAT A BROODJE BAL Natuurlijk Smullen (the organic snackbar), Jan van Galenstraat 78 (Recommended by Rogier van de Swag, snackshop fiend extraordinaire). www.natuurlijksmullen.nl

EXPERIENCE DUTCH CHEESE AT ITS FINEST The Kaas Kamer, Runstraat 7 (ask for Luuk). www.kaaskamer.nl

The rest, my friends, is up to you. Bonne voyage!

NOTES

WHERE WOULD JOHN GO?

John inspired us to spread the love, so spread the love we do. We exist to spread John's values as far and wide as we can with a couple of things very close to John's heart: wine and cookies. Everything that goes into them is 100% natural and is made with as little impact on the environment as possible. And of course they taste good. Damn good. We like to think that's what John would have wanted. You can find your nearest purveyor of Altman goodness at www.johnaltman.org

Thank you:
The Georgi family, the Gummo family, and Tom Godfrey for his help with the text.

Love,
Will